D1408747

KINDLE FIRE HDX

USERS MANUAL

The ultimate Kindle Fire guide to getting started, advanced tips, and finding unlimited free books, videos and apps on Amazon and beyond

By Steve Weber

All Rights Reserved © 2014 by Stephen W. Weber

No part of this book may be reproduced or transmitted in any form by any means, graphic, electronic, or mechanical, including photocopying, recording, taping or by any information storage or retrieval system, without permission in writing from the publisher.

The information in this book is offered with the understanding that it does not contain legal, financial, or other professional advice. Individuals requiring such services should consult a competent professional. The author and publisher make no representations about the suitability of the information contained in this book for any purpose. This material is provided "as is" without warranty of any kind.

Although every effort has been made to ensure the accuracy of the contents of this book, errors and omissions can occur. The publisher assumes no responsibility for any damages arising from the use of this book, or alleged to have resulted in connection with this book.

This book is not completely comprehensive. Some readers may wish to consult additional books for advice. This book is not authorized or endorsed by any company mentioned in the text.

Published by Stephen W. Weber
Printed in the United States of America
Weber Books   www.WeberBooks.com
ISBN: 978-1-936560-18-9

Free Kindle books, all you can eat!

Kindle Buffet is a daily website that features a hand-picked list of great Kindle books being offered free that day. Includes mysteries, romance, science-fiction, horror, non-fiction and more. Today's bestsellers and yesterday's classics. You may never need to pay for a book again! See for yourself by visiting www.KindleBuffet.com

kindle buffet!
Free books, all you can eat!

Allison (A Kane Novel)

Mystery, Thriller & Suspense
Author: Steve Gannon

Allison Kane, a journalism student at UCLA, takes a summer job as a TV news intern—soon becoming involved in a scandalous murder investigation and the media firestorm that follows—a position that pits her squarely against her iron-fisted police detective father.

Cafenova (Clairmont Series)

Christian Fiction > Romance
Author: S. Jane Scheyder

Leaving her broken heart behind in Seattle, Maddy Jacobs starts a new life on the coast of Maine. Although running a Bed and Breakfast has always been her dream, restoring the sprawling Victorian inn is a massive undertaking. Her contractor, competent, handsome, and built like a Greek god, could be the answer to her prayers. If she can keep her wits about her, she might just survive the summer.

20 Things I've Learned as an Entrepreneur

Small Business & Entrepreneurship
Author: Alicia Morga

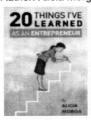

20 Things I've Learned as an Entrepreneur is the summary of lessons leading female technology entrepreneur Alicia Morga learned as a first-time entrepreneur in Silicon Valley. If you're an entrepreneur or if you've only dreamed about starting your own business, this quick important read is for you.

3 2135 00124 5865

Contents

Introduction

Amazon's Kindle Fire is a very affordable tablet computer—perhaps the best value in consumer electonics today. It runs on the Android operating system and, because of that, there is a wide variety of applications—called "apps"—available for it that expand its potential enormously.

Even more important, the Kindle Fire is a portal to Amazon.com's unparalled library of entertainment and educational content—an endless stream of books, magazines, movies, TV shows and games for people of every age and interest. And don't forget about the Internet. All of it is conveniently at your fingertips at great prices, and often absolutely free.

Kindle Fire has a touch-screen interface, which means that there's no bulky keyboard or mouse to fuss with. It has a brilliant, full-color display for video, and it doubles as a fine e-reader, music player, web-surfing tool, game machine, and much more. Kindle Fire HDX offers enormous utility at an amazing price.

Versus e-Ink Readers

E-ink readers use a particulate substance to form letters that are almost identical—some say even nicer to look at—than real ink on paper. The Kindle Fire, however, uses pixels, just like a regular computer screen with glorious full color. This makes the Kindle Fire more suitable for multimedia use and for reading full-color publications like graphic novels and magazines.

Versus Tablet Computers

The iPad is what many people think of first when it comes to tablet computers. But compared to the Kindle Fire, the iPad has some real disadvantages.

The iPad's hefty price is the first big drawback. And what do iPad buyers get for their extra money? Not much, it seems—their horsepower and picture quality have been eclipsed by the Kindle Fire HDX.

Kindle Fire has a default interface that makes it very Amazon-centric, but in this book you'll learn how to expand its horizons by accessing a universe of free apps and books that Amazon would rather keep a secret. Yes, your Amazon Kindle Fire can do just about anything that any other Android device can do, and that's quite a lot.

Amazon Prime

The Kindle Fire is equipped with a quad-core processor, giving it plenty of speed. And while it does have some limitations, the Kindle Fire also has a lot to offer. A big part of the Kindle's value equation is Amazon Prime, Amazon's annual membership program. Prime gives you access to a huge library of free movies and TV shows, similar to the Netflix service. You'll receive a one-month free trial of Prime in exchange for purchasing your Kindle Fire.

Second, Prime allows you to borrow one Kindle book every month with no due dates. These books come from the Kindle Lending Library. Not all books are included in the Lending Library, but many popular books are. If you're an avid reader, the Kindle Lending Library will pay off for you quite handsomely.

Third, aside from the Kindle experience, Prime gives you free and reduced-price shipping when your order physical products from Amazon. You'll get free two-day delivery of many items—and overnight shipping for just a few dollars more on any Prime-eligible item—a wonderful perk if you're a frequent Amazon shopper.

Your Head in the Cloud Drive

Perhaps you haven't heard about it yet, but as an Amazon customer you have access to a wireless storage system called the "Amazon Cloud." It serves as your personal, automatic hard drive in the sky, and it comes in quite handy for managing your digital library.

Each time you purchase digital content from Amazon—books, music, videos, apps and other documents—a permanent backup copy is stored for you in the Cloud for free. You can also use the Cloud to store your personal photos, videos and music on Amazon's secure servers—for easy access using your Kindle Fire and other devices.

You can view and download content from the Cloud any time you're connected to a WiFi network. To view your Cloud content, tap a content library (**Books**, for example) from the top navigation bar on your Kindle Fire's Home screen, then tap **Cloud**. Also, music files in the Cloud can be downloaded and streamed using the Cloud Player through its Web interface. See www.amazon.com/cloudplayer

Your Cloud Drive comes with 5 gigabytes (GB) of free storage, which is enough to hold about 1,000 songs. If you need more storage space, you can get it for a reasonable monthly fee.

One important detail: the digital content you buy from Amazon—music, video and e-books—don't count against your 5-GB limit. Your purchases are always backed up and available free in the Cloud.

1 ▶ FAST START GUIDE

The Kindle Fire is an advanced e-reader with extensive multimedia capabilities. The device utilizes a touch-screen for an input device. It has a 1/8" headphone/speaker jack on the side of the device. The wall charger port doubles as a USB connection to your computer.

If you're familiar with Kindle devices or tablet computers already, the setup process will be easy. Verify that your packaging contains your Kindle Fire and a wall socket charger. Remove the device from the plastic cover, plug the appropriate end of the charger cord into the Kindle, and the other end into the wall socket. Charging should take between 3 and 4 hours to complete fully, though this may vary.

When you turn it on for the first time, your Kindle Fire will walk you through your initial setup and demonstrate basic navigation. Provided you have an Amazon account already, setup should take less than 5 minutes. The full procedure is detailed below, in case you've inherited your Kindle Fire from another user, or you don't have an Amazon account.

A Quick Tour of Your New Kindle Fire

Getting started is simple enough. Here's how to control your Kindle Fire by using its touchscreen and hardware buttons:

- Turn on your Kindle by pressing the power button on the back. The screen illuminates.

- Unlock the screen by pressing and dragging the lock icon toward the left.

- Adjust the volume by pressing the + or — button on the back.

- Charge the battery by connecting the USB cable to the side of your Kindle as shown, and connect the other end of the cable to your Kindle wall charger.

VOLUME UP / DOWN

HEADPHONE / INPUT   REAR CAMERA

POWER BUTTON

USB PORT

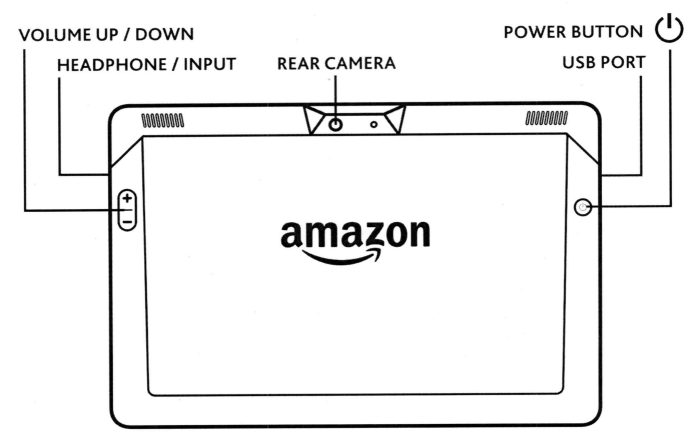

Above: The rear view of the Kindle Fire HDX. (Only the larger 8.9-inch Kindle Fire HDX has the rear-facing camera for taking pictures; the 7-inch model has only a front-facing camera.)

FRONT CAMERA

SLIDE TO UNLOCK

USB CABLE

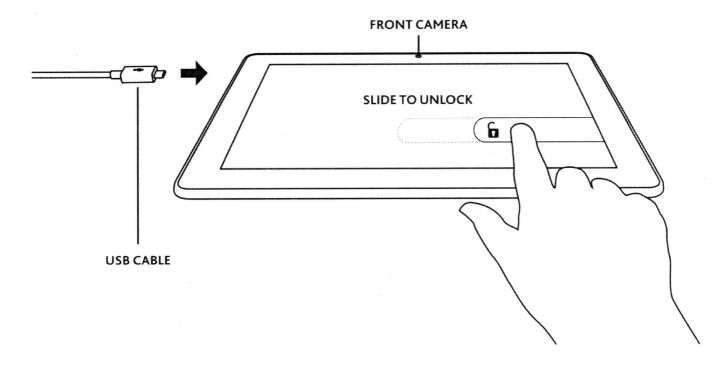

Above: Unlock your Kindle Fire by dragging your finger leftward across the screen.

Find the Home Screen

The **Home screen** on your Kindle Fire is the starting point for just about everything you'll do with the device. You can switch to the Home screen by tapping the icon ⌂ at the bottom of your screen. If you're currently running an application, you may have to exit it using the Left Arrow ⬅ .

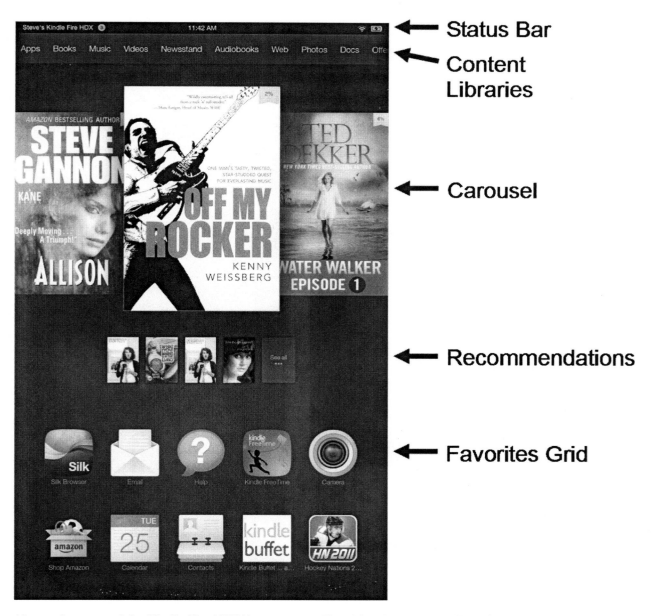

Above: Anatomy of the Kindle Fire HDX Home screen. To add an item to your Favorites, press and hold the item, then tap "Add to Home" from the pop-up menu. To remove an item, tap and hold them item and tap "Remove."

The **Home** screen displays your **Carousel** of recently used and favorite content and apps. The Home screen is a convenient place to search for content. At the very top of the screen is the **Status Bar**, which displays the "Name" of your Kindle Fire, the number of unread notifications, the wireless connection indicator, and the battery charge indicator.

Initiating an action on your Kindle Fire HDX often requires you to begin at the Home screen.

Above: The Status Bar, located at the top of the Kindle Fire's screen, displays your device name, the number of unread notifications, the time, wireless connection status, and a battery charge indicator.

Understand 'Portrait Mode' and 'Landscape Mode'

The layout of your Kindle Fire's screen depends on how your device is oriented. Rotate the device horizontally to switch to **Landscape Mode**, or vertically to switch to **Portrait Mode**.

To explain it a different way, with **Landscape Mode**, your screen is wider than it is tall, like a movie screen. With **Portrait mode**, your screen is taller than it is wide, like the shape of a mirror on a medicine chest.

Landscape mode

Portrait mode

Lock Your Screen's Orientation

By default, the Kindle Fire rotates into Landscape or Portrait modes automatically, depending on how the device is positioned in your hands. To lock your device into its current mode:

1. Swipe down from the top of the screen to reveal **Quick Settings**.
2. Tap **Auto-Rotate** to activate the **Locked** option.

Register Your Kindle Fire

Unless you received your Kindle Fire as a gift, you likely purchased it from Amazon yourself and it was already linked to your Amazon account when you opened the box. In that case, you can skip this section. Otherwise, follow this registration procedure:

1. From the Home screen, swipe downward from the top of the screen to reach **Quick Settings**. Tap **Settings**.

2. Tap **My Account**.

   • To use an existing Amazon account: enter its associated email address and password. Tap **Register**.

   • If you don't have an Amazon account: Tap **Create Account**, then follow the instructions on your screen to establish a new account.

Navigate Your Kindle Fire

Your **Home** screen shows your **Carousel** (the upper part of the screen with the large icons), which displays your recently used books, games, videos, music, apps and other digital content. To remove an item from the Carousel, press and hold the item, then tap **Remove from Carousel**.

To add your favorite apps and other content to your Home screen, press and hold the item, then tap **Add to Home**.

To access the items below the Carousel, drag the Carousel upward with a swipe of your finger. Return to the Carousel by swiping down.

While you're using your Kindle Fire, your main navigation tools are the **Home Button**, the **Back Arrow** to return to the previous screen, and the **Menu Button**.

• Go to **Home** by tapping

• Go to the previous screen by tapping

• Open the **Menu** by tapping

• Close the on-screen keyboard by tapping

Using the Navigation Bar

The top of your Home screen, below the Status Bar, is the **Navigation Bar**, which you can use to search for content and to access content libraries such as Games, Apps, Books, Music, Video and more.

Above: Your Navigation Bar appears at the top of your Home screen.

After you've tapped to open a content library, like Books, swipe from the left edge of the screen (or tap the icon in the top-left corner) to open the **Navigation Panel** and view selections for shopping and accessing content. The selections on the Navigation Panel depend on what type of content you're viewing.

Above: From within a content library (in this instance, Books), swiping from the left edge of the screen reveals a Navigation Panel and selections for shopping and accessing content.

Navigate With the Options Bar

At any Kindle Fire screen (with the exception of the Home screen), you can access the **Options Bar** (pictured above on the right edge of the screen). The Options Bar contains the **Back** icon ![Back icon], which enables you to retrace your steps to the previous screen. The **Home** screen icon returns you to the Home screen, and the **Search** icon lets you search for content on your device, in the Amazon store, or on the Web. Lastly, there's the **Menu** icon , which provides access to several functions and settings, depending on which content library you're using.

If the **Options Bar** isn't visible, tap the center of the screen (or tap the Handle icon) and the Options Bar appears.

Switch Between Recent Content With 'Quick Switch'

Quick Switch enables you to switch between recently used books, apps, video and music. In portrait mode, drag your finger up from the **Options Bar** at the bottom of your screen, then tap the item you want to open. (In landscape mode, the Options Bar will be on the right of your screen. Drag your finger leftward.)

If you're viewing an app in full-screen mode, the Options Bar isn't visible. In that case, drag your finger from the **Handle** icon, , to reveal Quick Switch.

Understand 'List View' and 'Grid View'

When you open a Content Library, such as Books, you can view your purchased items in both a **list view** and a **grid view**. The grid view presents you with thumbnail images of the covers of your books and magazines, while the list view shows smaller thumbnails but more written detail. Tap the **Menu Button**, , to switch between list view and grid view.

Manage Your Payment Settings

All of your transactions with Amazon via the Kindle Fire require a valid payment setting, even if you are downloading a free item. To view or change your payment setting:

1. Visit "Manage Your Kindle" (www.amazon.com/myk) and click **Kindle Payment Settings**.

2. Click **Edit**. This will launch the **Your Default 1-Click payment setting** page, where you can edit the settings.

3. Select your credit card information and click **Continue**. If desired, you can add a new card.

4. Enter your billing address and click **Continue**. You'll arrive at the **Kindle Payment Settings** page, where you can view your edited 1-Click payment method.

Sync Across Kindle Fire and Apps

Amazon's **Whispersync** feature enables you to synchronize all your Kindle content to all your devices and Kindle apps, including your books, audiobooks, personal documents, games, and Amazon Instant Video. For example, if you stop reading a book on your Kindle Fire at the end of chapter one, the book will automatically open at the same point on all of your other Kindle devices and apps. Whispersync also makes your annotations available to all your devices, including bookmarks, highlights and notes.

Whispersync is enabled by default. To change the setting:

1. Visit Manage Your Kindle at www.amazon.com/myk

2. Under **Your Kindle Account**, click **Manage Your Devices**.

3. Under Device Synchronization (Whispersync Settings), tap the button for **Whispersync Device Synchronization** (on or off).

TIP: To ensure your progress through a book is recorded accurately, tap the **Home** icon , when you finish reading. Then, if you resume reading on a different device or app, the document will automatically open at the place you left off.

Connect to a Wi-Fi Network

For most Kindle Fire users, Wi-Fi is the primary Internet connection. Your Kindle automatically finds nearby networks and displays their name. Some networks, such as those in coffee shops and restaurants, are free for anyone to use, and don't require a password. Home Wi-Fi networks and some others usually require a password.

1. Swipe down from the top of your screen to show **Quick Settings**, then tap **Wireless**.

2. Ensure that **Airplane Mode** is switched **Off**.

3. Tap **Wi-Fi**.

4. Beside **Wi-Fi**, tap **On**.

5. Tap a network to join it. If the network listing shows a "lock" icon, it requires a password. Enter the network's password and tap **Connect**.

In the future, your Kindle Fire will find and connect the networks you've joined previously. The wireless indicator is located on the top-right corner of your Kindle Fire, next to the battery indicator. A display of four bars indicates that your device is connected to a network with a strong signal. An "X" over the bar icon indicates your Kindle Fire isn't connected to the Internet. A display of no bars indicates your Kindle Fire is not connected to Wi-Fi.

Trouble Connecting to a Wi-Fi Network

If you're unable to connect to a home network you've used previously, follow this procedure:

1. Press and hold your Kindle Fire's **Power** button, then tap **Power off**.

2. Turn off your Wi-Fi router and modem. Wait 30 seconds.

3. Turn on your modem and wait while it restarts.

4. Turn on your router; wait for it to restart.

5. Press and hold your Kindle Fire's **Power** button for two or three seconds. After your device restarts, try connecting to your Wi-Fi network again.

Connect to a Mobile Network

You can connect to mobile networks operated by Verizon and AT&T if you purchased a Kindle Fire model with mobile service. If you see one of the mobile indicators on the status bar—4G, 3G, EDGE or GPRS—your device is already connected.

A data plan is required to connect to a mobile network. If you're not already an AT&T or Verizon customer, you'll need to create a new account on your device to access wireless. For updated information about the data plans available, visit AT&T's website at www.att.com/shop/wireless/data-plans.html or Verizon at www.verizonwireless.com/wcms/consumer/shop/shop-data-plans.html

Your Kindle Fire automatically switches to Wi-Fi when available. If you're out of range of Wi-Fi, your device switches to a mobile connection when enabled.

1. Swipe down from the top of the screen to reveal **Quick Settings**, then tap Wireless.

2. Tap **Mobile Network**.

3. Beside **Mobile Network**, tap **On**.

To set up a data plan, while connected to Wi-Fi:

1. Swipe down from the top of the screen to reveal **Quick Settings**, then tap **Wireless**.

2. Tap **Mobile Network**, then tap **Manage Data Plan**. Your Web browser will launch at your wireless provider's website.

3. Follow the on-screen instructions to complete setting up your account.

Using the Keyboard

If you have a smartphone or other touch-screen device, you're probably already familiar with the basics of a touch-screen keyboard. If you're not, the learning curve shouldn't be too steep, but there may be some frustration initially. Here are some basic tips to keep in mind.

• It's much easier to type accurately if your Kindle is in landscape mode—the keyboard is enlarged, giving you more room to type.

• Use your thumbs to type while holding the Kindle Fire in your hand.

• A screen protector can prevent fingerprint smudges from building up on your screen resulting from typing.

• Your keyboard will autocorrect words for you, but you can turn this feature off, which may actually be more desirable. To turn off auto-correction:

1. Swipe down from the top of the screen to reveal **Quick Settings**.

2. Tap **Settings**.

3. Tap **Language & Keyboard**.

4. Set **Auto-Correction Off**.

Changing the Settings

To access the various settings controls on your Kindle Fire, swipe your finger from the top of the screen downward. The following menu appears at the top of your screen. (We will review each of these setting options in detail later):

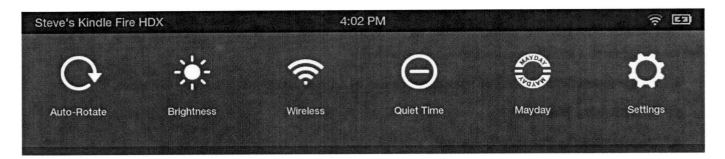

Above: The Quick Settings menu

Charge Your Battery

By using the supplied USB cable and power adapter, your Kindle Fire should fully charge within a few hours. If you use a different power adapter, however, your charging time will lengthen.

While your Kindle Fire is charging, the battery icon at the top of the device shows a lightning bolt, . If the lightning bolt is absent, your device is not charging.

TIP: Your Kindle Fire uses a lithium ion battery. Battery performance can degrade at extreme temperatures. Batteries discharge faster in cold temperatures, so warm up your device before turning it on in cold environments. Avoid leaving your Kindle in a car in the summertime or other extremely hot environments, which can cause permanent battery damage.

Fix a Frozen or Slow Screen

Similar to a computer, sometimes your Kindle Fire may freeze up, requiring a reboot. To restart your device:

1. Press and hold the power button for two or three seconds until the message appears: "Do you want to shut down your Kindle?" Tap **Power Off**.

2. After your device has fully turned off, restart it by pressing the power button.

If your device remains slow after restarting, try this resetting procedure, which forces the device to power off: Connect your Kindle to a power adapter, then press and hold the power button for a full 20 seconds. The device will shut down. Then press the power button to restart.

Getting Help from Amazon

If you need to contact Amazon's customer support staff, click the "Contact Us" button on the right side of any help page, such as www.Amazon.com/help and then choose your preferred method of contact, such as "phone," "email" or "c hat." Using the contact form automatically informs Amazon's staff who you are, and it saves you the trouble of having to confirm your identify.

If you'd rather phone Amazon direct, the numbers are:

U.S. and Canada: 1-866-216-1072
Spanish Support: 866-749-7538
International: 1-206-266-2992

Connect to Amazon Tech Support Via the Mayday Button

Tapping the **Mayday** button on the Kindle Fire's **Quick Settings** menu establishes a video and audio connection to an Amazon technical advisor who can guide you through any support issues. The tech advisor can assist you by drawing on your screen, explaining how to accomplish something for yourself, or the tech advisor can do it for you.

Mayday is available 24 hours a day, seven days a week. During your session, you'll be able to see the tech advisor on your screen, but they won't see you.

1. Swipe down from the top of the screen to access **Quick Settings**. Tap **Mayday** to open **Amazon Assist**.

2. Tap **Connect**.

3. To turn off the session, tap the **Mayday** button and swipe from the left edge of the screen. Tap **Settings**, then **Off**.

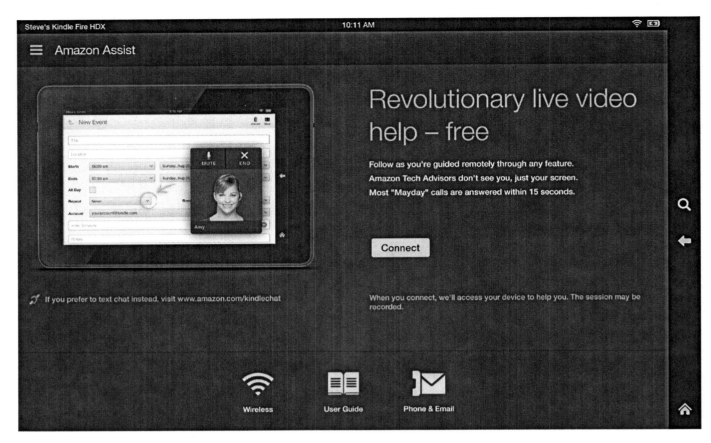

Above: Tapping the "Mayday" button from the Quick Settings menu opens "Amazon Assist," where you can connect to an Amazon tech advisor for assistance.

2 ► SURF THE WEB

One of the best features of the Kindle Fire is its snappy performance in web browsing. The Fire's "Silk" browser harnesses your device's processor and Amazon's Cloud to make your Internet experience as fast and smooth as possible—like silk. Don't hesitate to tilt your Kindle over to landscape orientation, which often makes typing and navigating the web easier.

Getting on the Internet couldn't be easier. Go to your **Home** screen and select **Web** from the navigation menu. This will launch the browser. Or you can tap the **Silk** icon (which is included the "favorites" section at the bottom of your Home screen). When the browser opens for the first time, you'll see a quick tutorial demonstrating its basic features. Tap **OK** to exit the tutorial. To search for a different website, tap the **Address Bar** to search and tap **Go**. If you know the address, such as www.amazon.com , type it in the address bar.

Other navigation tools associated with the Silk Browser are found in the **Options** bar located along the right edge of the screen. (If the **Options** bar isn't visible, tap the **Handle** icon .)

Zoom In or Out

To get a closer look at a website, you can zoom in by tapping on the center of the screen. This automatically resizes the page so that the main portion fills your screen. Another way to zoom in (or out) is by spreading or "pinching" two fingers along the touch-screen. Here's how: to zoom in, place two of your fingers in the center of the screen and then spread them apart, moving your fingers toward the edges of the screen. You might think of this gesture as grabbing onto the webpage and stretching it outward. Practice this a couple of times to get a feel for it. The opposite gesture—an inward, pinching motion—enables you to zoom out.

- **Search for a website** – Tap the **Search** icon and enter your search terms.

- **Add a new tab** – Tap . You can create up to 10 tabs. Close a tab by tapping the X in the tab.

- **Go to the previous page** – Tap the **Back Button** .

- **Go to the most recent page you've visited** – Tap the **Forward Button** .

- **Enter enlarge the web browser to take up the entire screen** – Tap the **Full-Screen Button** . To exit full-screen mode, tap the **handle** icon .

- **To share page, add bookmarks, find in page, and more** – Tap the **Menu** ▤ **Button**.

Enjoy Reading View

If you regularly read the content on websites, you know how distracting advertisements and other Internet doodads can be. Fortunately, Amazon's Silk browser has a **Reading View** that strips out most graphics and advertisements, so you can read without the extra stuff.

- To Switch to Reading View, tap the **Reading View** ⟨👓 Reading view⟩ button (when available).

- To change the font size, background color, margins, and text alignment, tap **Aa**.

- To exit Reading View, tap the **X**.

Bookmarking Web Pages

Bookmarking web pages is easy. When you're at a URL that you want to bookmark, tap the **Menu Button** ▤ , then **Add Bookmark**.

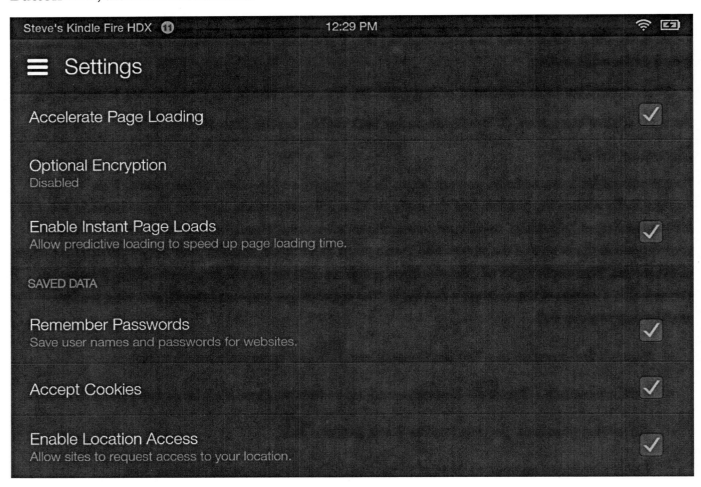

Above: The Silk browser's default settings

To edit your bookmarks, tap the **Menu Button** [icon] , then tap **Edit Bookmark**.

Here's an explanation of the Silk browser's settings:

Search Engine: By default, Bing is selected. You can change the setting to Yahoo! or Google.

Block pop-up windows: To make Silk notify you when a pop-up window is detected, tap **Ask**. Your other options are to **Never** block a pop-up, or **Always** block them.

Accelerate page loading: Allow Silk to use the Amazon Cloud to speed web page loading.

Optional Encryption: Tap this option to scramble requests routed through Amazon's servers. (May slow down web page loading.

Enable instant page loads: Allows the Silk browser to predict the next page you're likely to visit and prepare it for loading, enabling faster web surfing.

Clear Browser data: Enhance your privacy by deleting your browsing history, including websites you've visited, saved passwords, and personal information added to forms.

- To clear browser data for a certain website, tap **Individual Website Data**, then tap the website to clear your data.

- Periodically clearing your browser data ensures a faster browsing experience.

Accept Cookies: Cookies enable you to save user information for certain websites. They are enabled by default, but you can turn them off and on.

Enable location: Some websites use your location data to customize your browsing experience. When a website requests your location, Silk prompts you to **Allow** or **Decline**. Allowing will pull up information that's closer to where you actually are. It's very handy if you're traveling with your Kindle.

Web Privacy Settings and Options

You can customize how the Silk web browser behaves. To access the settings while using Silk, swipe from the left edge of the screen and tap **Settings**.

Several of the web browser settings control the security or privacy aspects of the browser. The **Remember Passwords** setting, for instance, determines whether the browser will automatically fill in your password on restricted sites. If you're worried about security, be sure to uncheck the checkbox. Otherwise, anyone who picks up your Kindle Fire can access websites for which you've previously entered the password.

3 ► HOW TO READ A BOOK, KINDLE STYLE

When most people think of a "Kindle," they think of an e-reader. Before the Fire came along, that's about all you could do with an e-reader—read books. Back then, most e-readers came with a black-and-white display called e-ink. The older models—which are still quite popular— don't emit any light.

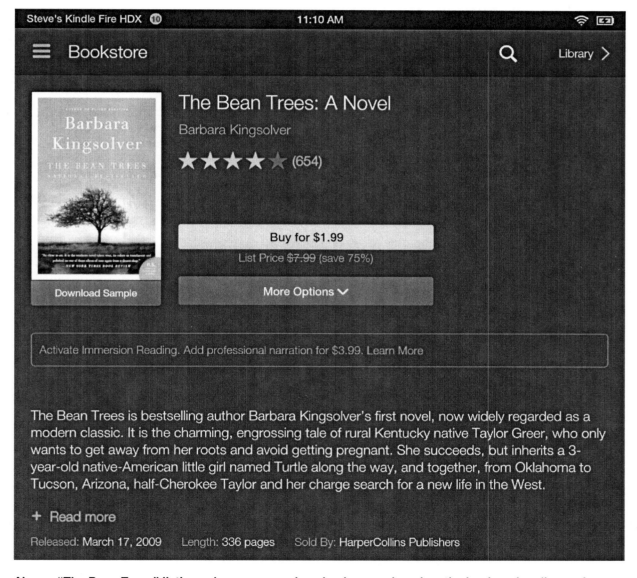

Above: "The Bean Trees" listing, where you can download a sample or buy the book and audio versions.

The Kindle Fire, however, functions more like a computer monitor—generating its own light of varying colors. The reading experience is quite different, but the Fire functions quite nicely as an e-reader that can handle old-fashioned black-and-white books as well as graphic novels and full-color magazines. And although there are zillions of Kindle e-books from which to choose, books are only the tip of the iceberg when it comes to reading on your Kindle.

Buy and Download Books, Magazines and Newspapers

After you establish your wireless connection, you can buy books, magazines and newspapers from the Kindle store for download directly to your Kindle Fire.

The Newsstand section of your Kindle Fire offers a vast array of magazines and newspapers. You can buy single issues, or buy a regular subscription.

1. To visit the Kindle store, tap **Books** or **Newsstand** in the top navigation bar of the Home screen. Then tap **Store**.

2. After you've selected a title:

    - Tap the **Buy** button to purchase a book or single newspaper or magazine issue.

    - Tap the **Subscribe Now** button to subscribe to a newspaper or magazine.

Alternatively, you can use a desktop computer to browse the Kindle Store. During the checkout process, select which Kindle device you want the content delivered to from the drop-down list.

If you're unsure of a purchase, tap **Download Sample** to download the beginning of the book for free. At the conclusion of the sample, tap **Buy for ...** if you wish to purchase the book. Unlike complete Kindle books, samples aren't stored in the Amazon Cloud and don't sync across Kindle devices or reading applications.

After you've purchased a book, magazine or newspaper, it automatically downloads to your Kindle Fire. The item is also stored in your Kindle Library, ready for downloading to other Kindle devices and reading apps registered to the same account.

Items more than seven issues old are automatically deleted from your device in order to conserve storage space, but exceptions are possible. For example, if you'd like a magazine to remain on your device after the default storage period, tap and hold the magazine's cover in your library. From the menu that pops up, select "Keep". This will ensure that it is not automatically erased from your device.

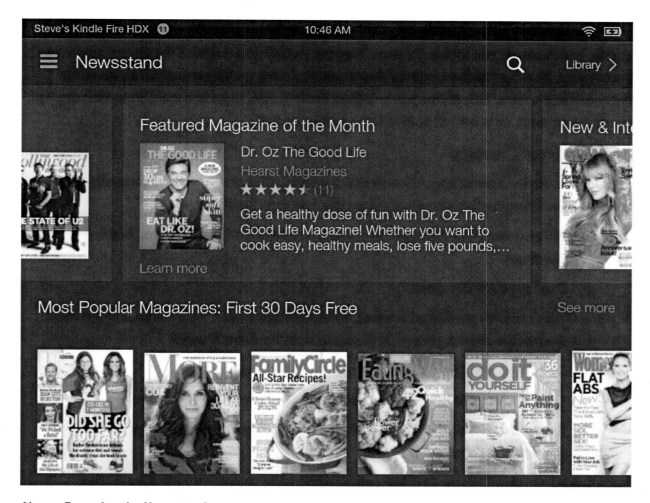

Above: Browsing the Newsstand

After you've accumulated back issues of more than one publication, issues will be sorted by title, enabling you to easily browse your library of that particular publication.

Magazines and newspapers can be displayed in two different ways. Tap the middle of the screen when you're reading a magazine or newspaper and an **Options** menu will appear. You can choose between **Text View** and **Page View** by clicking on the icon at the top right of the screen. **Text View** provides only the text of an article, while **Page view** shows you the magazine's original layout, including illustrations, just as it appeared on paper. You can adjust the size of the text by clicking the **Aa** icon.

TIP: Some magazines and newspapers don't come in the regular Newsstand format, but are instead provided as apps. If you want to purchase one of these, you have to buy the subscription in the Apps store and download the app to read the periodical. Many magazine apps are "free" but they only give you a portion of the magazine's content for free.

Like magazines, you can navigate your book library by tapping the right-hand side of the screen, which moves you forward a page. Tapping the left-hand side of the screen moves you back a page. You can tap the center of your screen to bring up the contextual menu at the bottom of the screen. This allows you to adjust the font size, to go to a specific section or page, to add a comment, or to search the book for particular text.

Undelivered Content

If you don't receive a book, app, video or other content after purchasing it, manually sync your device to check for pending downloads from the Amazon Cloud:

1. Swipe down from the top of the screen to access **Quick Settings**, then tap **Settings**.

2. Tap **Sync All Content**.

If you still don't receive purchased content, check to ensure you have a wireless connection. Also, double-check to ensure your 1-Click payment method is still valid:

1. Visit **Manage Your Kindle** at www.amazon.com/myk

2. Under **Your Kindle Account**, click **Kindle Payment Settings**.

3. Under **Your Default 1-Click Payment Method**, Click **Edit** to review or edit your 1-Click payment settings.

Sometimes a content delivery problem can be resolved by restarting your Kindle Fire:

1. Press and hold the **Power** button for a full 20 seconds. Your Kindle Fire will shut down while you hold the **Power** button.

2. After 20 seconds, release the **Power** button.

3. Press the **Power** button again to restart your Kindle Fire.

Reading Books and Personal Documents

The **Books** section of your library contains all of the e-books you've purchased from Amazon. Once you register your device, the titles and thumbnails of previously purchased books are downloaded. The entire text of the book isn't downloaded to your Kindle until you actually open the document. To open a book, simply tap on its cover thumbnail or—if you're viewing in list view—tap on the text next to the title.

You can sync your book between Kindle devices, add bookmarks to notes, and highlight text while you're reading Kindle books.

Sync to the Furthest Page Read

You can manually sync your Kindle Fire to the furthest page read for books you're reading on other Kindle devices or reading apps. Whispersync will automatically update and sync your books across all your registered devices and apps. If Whispersync is disabled, you can manually sync your book to the furthest page read.

1. While reading, tap the center of the screen.

2. Swipe from the left edge of the screen to open the **Go To** menu, then tap **Sync to Furthest Page read**.

To enable Whispersync to sync your furthest page read, bookmarks, highlights and notes:

1. Visit **Manage Your Kindle** at www.amazon.com/myk

2. Under **Your Kindle Account**, select **Manage Your Devices**.

3. Under **Device Synchronization (Whispersync Settings)**, ensure that **Whispersync Device Synchronization** is **ON**.

TIP: To ensure your progress through a book is recorded accurately, tap the **Home** icon when you reach a stopping point. Then, if you resume reading on a different device or app, the document will automatically open at the place you left off.

Find Other Locations in a Book

While reading a book, you can jump to a different place by using the **Go To** menu, or you can move quickly through the book using the progress bar.

*   To go to the next page, tap the right side of the screen.

*   To go to the previous page, tap the left side of the screen.

*   While reading, tap the center of the screen, then swipe from the left edge of the screen to open the **Go To** menu.

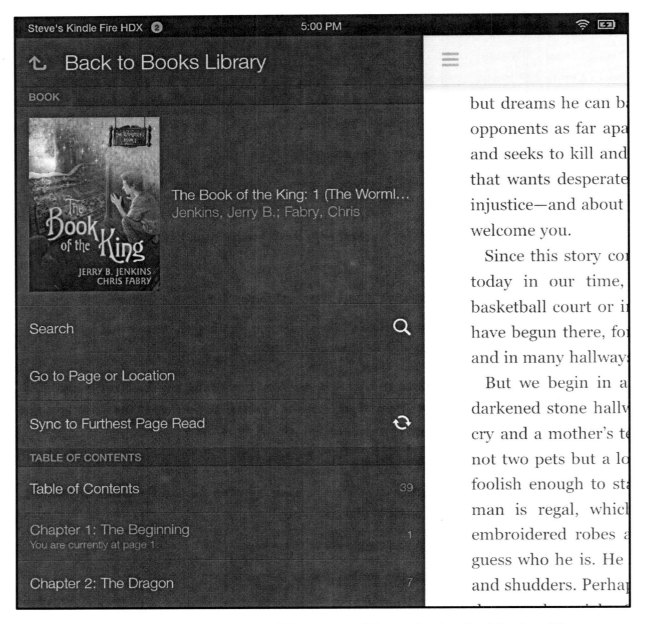

Above: While reading a book, tap the center of the screen and then swipe from the left edge of the screen to open the Go To menu.

In the **Go To** menu, tap:

- **Go to Page or Location** – Enter a page number or location to jump to it.

- **A chapter or section in the Table of Contents** – Scroll up or down until you see your desired chapter or section heading, then tap the heading to go to the first page of that chapter or section.

- **To scroll quickly through your book** – Tap the center of the screen to bring up the progress bar (shown in the illustration below), then press and drag the circle left or right.

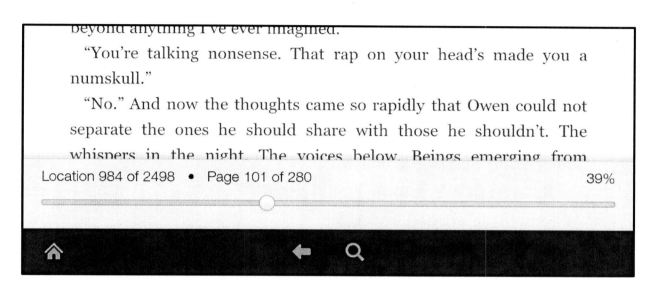

beyond anything I've ever imagined.

"You're talking nonsense. That rap on your head's made you a numskull."

"No." And now the thoughts came so rapidly that Owen could not separate the ones he should share with those he shouldn't. The whispers in the night. The voices below. Beings emerging from

Location 984 of 2498 • Page 101 of 280   39%

Above: To move quickly through large chunks of a book, tap the center of the screen to bring up the progress bar, which appears near the bottom of the screen. Then press and drag the circle left or right.

Change the Appearance of Text

With a regular paper-bound book, you're stuck with the typography chosen by the publisher. If the text is too small, you're simply out of luck—unless you have some reading glasses handy. With the Kindle Fire, however, you can change the font, line spacing, margins, or background color of a book to match your personal preferences.

1. While reading, tap the center of the screen to access the reading toolbar, then tap **Aa (view)**.

2. Change the text display for your Kindle book:

   - Font size – Tap **Aa** to increase the font size, or tap **Aa** to decrease the font size.

   - Font – Tap the font name (for example, **Georgia**), and then tap your preferred font.

3. Set the line spacing, margins, or background color:

   - **Background Color** – Select the color scheme for the background color. Choose **White** ▐ , **Sepia** ▐ , or **Black** ▐ backgrounds.

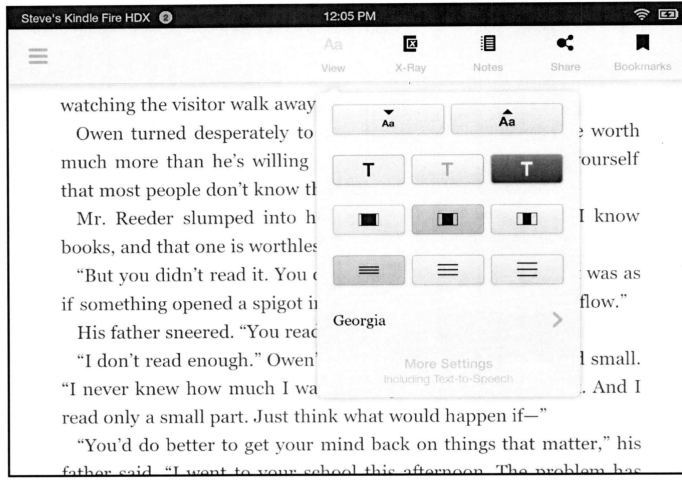

Above: Tap the center of the screen to access the reading toolbar, then tap Aa (View) to access text appearance settings.

- **Margins** – Select the amount of space to appear on the left and right sides of each page. Choose **Narrow** , **Normal** , or **Wide** margins.

- **Line Spacing** – Select the amount of space to appear above and below each line. Choose **Narrow** , **Normal** or **Wide** spacing.

- Unfortunately, you can't change the text appearance of PDFs.

View Your Reading Progress

With a paper-bound book, you have a simple reference point to judge your progress. By looking at the stack of pages, it's easy to see if you're halfway through a book, three-quarters of the way through, or somewhere in between. With Kindle books, you have three reference points—the number of "pages" read, the percentage of a book read, or the amount of time left in the chapter or book.

Location numbers – These are the digital equivalent of physical page numbers, and provide a way to easily reference a place in your reading material regardless of font size. The location displayed in a Kindle book is specific to the Kindle format and doesn't match the page number of printed editions.

Page numbers – These correspond to a book's printed edition. Not all Kindle books include page numbers. Because the font size and other elements are variable, it's possible to view more than one page (or less than a full page) on your screen at one time.

Time to Read – This feature uses your reading speed to calculate how much time is left before you finish your chapter or book.

While reading, tap the lower left corner of the screen to toggle between:

- Time left in chapter

- Time left in book

- Location numbers

- Page numbers (if available)

Tap the center of the screen to show the progress bar. Reading progress is displayed as a percentage.

Enjoy Enhanced Reading Features

One of the most popular features of the Kindle is its built-in dictionary, which is infinitely easier and faster than the old-fashioned method of grabbing a two- or three-pound dictionary off your bookshelf and thumbing through hundreds of pages to unearth a definition. And the built-in dictionary is just the beginning of the Kindle's enhanced reading features.

Look Up Words in the Dictionary or Wikipedia

While reading, you can look up words on your Kindle Fire from the built-in dictionaries or Wikipedia, the online encyclopedia, using the **Smart Lookup** feature.

The Kindle Fire comes with *The New Oxford American Dictionary* and *Oxford Dictionary of English.* If you wish, you can also download free dictionaries for French, Spanish, German, Italian, Brazilian Portuguese, Japanese, and simplified Chinese.

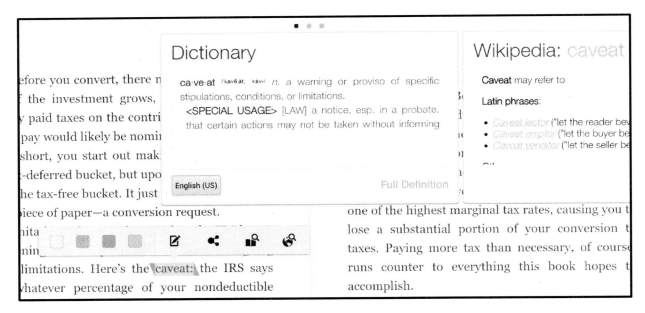

Above: Press and hold a word to reveal its dictionary and Wikipedia entries.

1. While reading, press and hold a word, then release to see the **Smart Lookup** cards.

   - **Dictionary**: Tap **Full Definition** to see more, or tap the language indicated in the definition box to choose another dictionary in a different language. Tap or swipe to turn pages within the dictionary.

   - **Wikipedia**: Swipe to the left to reveal the Wikipedia card. For more information, tap **Go to Wikipedia**.

2. Tap outside the cards to return to the book.

Translate Text Using Instant Translations

While reading, you can select text and use **Instant Translations** to translate the text to a different language.

1. While reading, press and drag to highlight text you want to translate.

2. Swipe to the left until you see the translation card.

3. To hear the pronunciation of the text, tap the Speak 🔊 button.

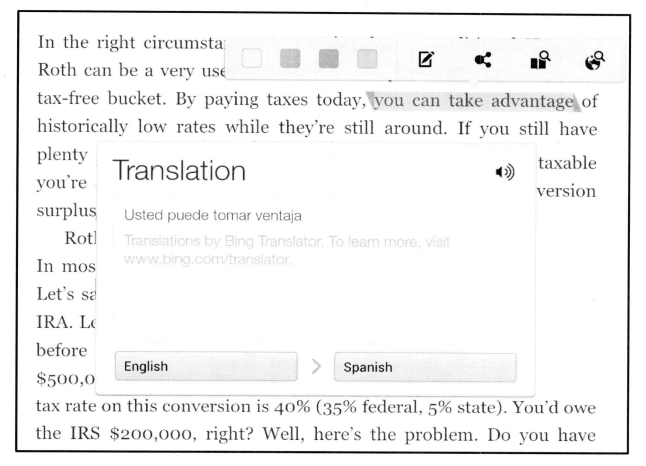

In the right circumsta[...] Roth can be a very use[...] tax-free bucket. By paying taxes today, you can take advantage of historically low rates while they're still around. If you still have plenty [...] taxable you're [...] version surplus [...]

Rot[...]

In mos[...]

Let's sa[...]

IRA. L[...]

before[...]

$500,0[...]

tax rate on this conversion is 40% (35% federal, 5% state). You'd owe the IRS $200,000, right? Well, here's the problem. Do you have

Translation

Usted puede tomar ventaja

Translations by Bing Translator. To learn more, visit www.bing.com/translator.

English > Spanish

Above: Press and drag text to reveal a translation into a different language.

Read and Listen Simultaneously With Immersion Reading

If you've never tried it, you'd be surprised how much more of a book you can absorb using Amazon's **Immersion Reading** feature, in which you listen to a audio narration of the book while simultaneously reading the text. To do it, you'll need to buy the Kindle book plus the matching audiobook version, and the title must be "Whispersync for Voice-ready," which is noted in Amazon's product description. For a list of books that support Immersion Reading, visit www.amazon.com/store/whispersyncvoice

1. To activate Immersion Reading:

   • **If you already own the title**: From the **Books** library, tap **Store**, then search for the book you currently own. On the product detail page for the Kindle book, tap **Add Narration** to purchase the identical audiobook version of your title, then tap **Download**.

- **If you don't own the title**: From the **Books** library, swipe from the left edge of the screen, and then tap **Immersion Reading**. From there, you can browse all titles in the Kindle store that support Immersion Reading. Tap the title to purchase the book, then activate Immersion Reading.

- To use Immersion Reading, open your Kindle book, then tap the center of the screen to open the reading toolbar at the bottom of the page. Tap the **Play** ▶ button to hear narration and see real-time highlighting of the text while you read.

Listen To Books With Text-to-Speech

If you can tolerate the somewhat robotic voice of **Text-to-Speech**, you can listen to a narration of most books, newspapers, magazines, blogs, and personal documents using your Kindle Fire. This feature isn't enabled on all Kindle books—if it is, you'll see **Text-to-Speech: Enabled** on Amazon's product page for the book.

1. While reading, tap the center of the screen, then tap **Aa (View).**

2. Tap **More Settings**, then tap **On** beside **Text-to-Speech**.

3. Tap the screen to reveal the progress bar, then tap the **Play** ▶ button beside the progress bar to listen to spoken text. To increase or decrease the speed of the Text-to-Speech voice, tap the **Narration Speed** button.

See More of Your Book With X-Ray

X-Ray lets you explore the foundation and details of your book, and you can view more detailed information from Wikipedia and Shelfari, Amazon's community-maintained encyclopedia for book readers. X-Ray isn't available for all Kindle books—if it's not, the X-Ray button is unavailable.

1. While reading, tap the center of the screen, then tap **X-Ray**.

2. Sort and filter the list of topics:

   - To sort, tap **By Relevance**, **In order of Appearance**, or **Alphabetical**.

   - To filter by the type of topic, tap **All**, **People**, or **Terms**.

The bars show all of the locations in the page, chapter or book where the character or word is mentioned.

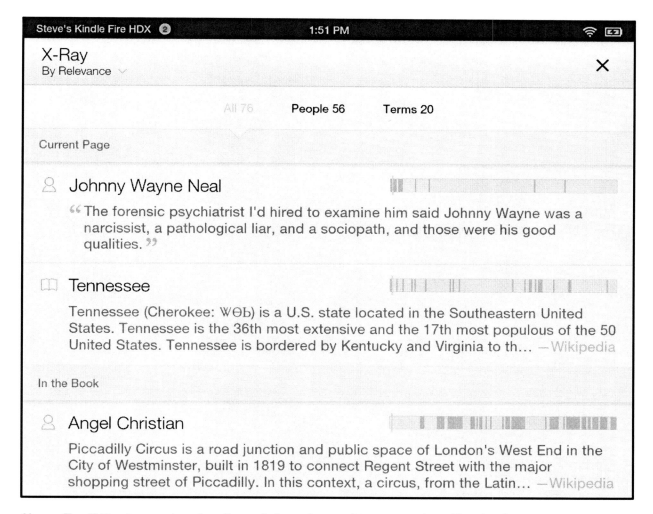

Above: Tap X-Ray to reveal explanations of characters and terms mentioned in a book.

Searching Within Books

Finding a needle in a haystack is as easy as falling off a log—if you're using your Kindle. The Search button, represented by the magnifying-glass icon on the right side of the screen, allows you to search for words or phrases. Here's how to perform a search:

1. Tap the center of the screen to call up the menu.

2. Tap the **Magnifying Glass** icon on the right edge of the screen.

3. Use the keyboard to enter your term(s) in the search field on the top of the screen.

4. Tap "**Go**" on the keyboard or the **Magnifying Glass** next to the search field.

Remember that the search function will find every single instance of the term or phrase you specify. If you search for a common word like "the" for instance, you'll get bogged down with a ton of references.

The search function is quite handy when you're using reference books, and it's smart too. For example, if you were searching for the word "antidisestablishmentarianism," you needn't type the whole thing. Just type "antidisest," and your target will show up.

To navigate from the search results to the text location where the word actually occurs, just tap the appropriate display in the search results.

Use Bookmarks, Highlights, and Notes

You can add or remove bookmarks at any location in a Kindle book or personal document.

1. **Add a bookmark**: Tap the top right corner of the screen. A Bookmark will appear.

2. **Remove a bookmark**: Tap the Bookmark .

To quickly view, navigate, add or remove bookmarks, tap the center of the screen, then tap **Bookmarks**. A preview window appears. Tap a bookmark in the preview window, and you'll arrive at that location in your book.

You can add or remove highlights at any location in a Kindle book or personal document.

1. **Highlight a word:** Press and hold the word, then tap your preferred color.

2. **Highlight a phrase:** Press and drag to highlight the text, then tap your preferred color. Drag the handles at the start or end of the highlighted text to edit your highlight. If the phrase you're highlighting spans multiple pages, press and drag to highlight to the bottom right corner of the screen, and the page will turn, with the highlight automatically continuing to the first period on the following page.

3. **Remove a highlight:** Press and hold a word in the highlighted area, then tap the X in the color previously selected.

4. **View Popular Highlights:** Tap the center of the screen, tap **Aa** (view), then tap **More Options**. Tap **On** to turn on **Popular Highlights**. You'll see a dashed underline of the Popular Highlights, which tallies the highlights of all Kindle customers and identifies the most-often passages highlighted.

Add, Edit or Remove Notes

You can add **Notes** at any location in a Kindle book or personal document.

- **Add a note:**

a) Press and drag to highlight the text.

b) Tap the **Note** 📝 icon, then type your note.

Tap **Save** to create your note. A notepad 📄 icon appears in the passage where you made the note.

- **Edit a note:**

(a) Tap the notepad 📄 icon where the note appears.

(b) After you edit your note, tap **Save**.

- **Remove a note:**

(a) Tap the notepad 📄 icon where the note appears, then tap **Delete**.

Buy and Download Audiobooks

In the audiobooks library on your Kindle Fire, you can buy and download audiobooks from Audible.com, a division of Amazon.

1. From **Home**, tap **Audiobooks**, then tap **Store**.

2. Use the search box to find a title. You can narrow your search by swiping from the left edge of your screen and select a category, such as **Audible Best Sellers**.

3. Tap a title to listen to a sample of the narration and see purchase options. If you're an Audible member, you can buy the audiobook with your credits. If you don't have an Audible membership and you'd just like to buy the audiobook without signing up for membership, tap **Buy for...**

4. To listen, from your **Home** screen, tap **Audiobooks**. Tap a title to download it to your Kindle.

Manage Your Library

After you've accumulated dozens, or perhaps hundreds, of digital items, keeping track of it all might seem daunting. Fortunately, Amazon has a system that makes it simple. By visiting the "Manage Your Kindle" web page (www.amazon.com/myk), you can locate and deliver items from your Kindle Library to your Kindle devices or reading apps.

Deliver Items to Your Kindle

1. Visit "Manage Your Kindle" at www.amazon.com/myk

2. Under **Your Kindle Library**, locate the item you want to deliver.

3. Click **Actions**, then **Deliver to my ...**

4. Select the device or app from the drop-down menu at **Deliver to my...**

5. Click **Deliver**. Your book or other content will be sent to your Kindle Fire or reading app.

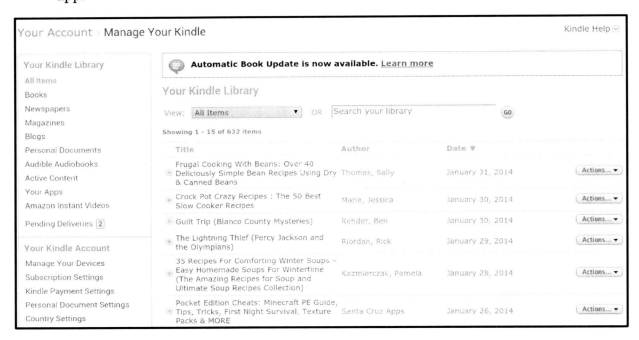

Above: The "Manage Your Kindle" web page at www.amazon.com/myk

Delete Content From Your Kindle Fire

To free up storage space on your Kindle Fire, you can remove items from the device. Digital content from Amazon remains saved to the Cloud and can be downloaded again in the future.

1. Swipe down from the top of the screen to view **Quick Settings**, then tap **Settings**.

2. Tap **Device**, then tap **Storage**.

a) Tap **1-Tap Archive** to eliminate items that have not been used recently. This feature organizes your infrequently used items and enables you to remove all of them from your device by tapping **Archive**.

b) Tap a content category from the list to see file names and sixes. Mark the checkbox beside any items you'd like to remove, then tap **Remove**. Important programs are grouped into the System Applications and Systems folder, and these can't be modified or removed.

To remove apps, games or music from the Cloud permanently, go to the **Apps**, **Games or Music** library on your device, then tap **Cloud**. Press and hold the item you want to remove. Tap **Delete from Cloud**. To permanently remove books, magazines or newspapers from the Cloud, visit Manage Your Kindle at www.amazon.com/myk

Organize Your Content With Cloud Collections

You can arrange the content on your device into custom categories stored in the Cloud by using **Cloud Collections**. You can add as many items as you wish to each collection—including books, apps, games, audiobooks and personal documents. However, you cannot add music, videos, photos, newspapers or magazines to Cloud Collections.

- **Access a collection**: From the **Home** screen, tap a Kindle content library (**Books**, for example) in the top navigation bar. Swipe from the left edge of the screen, then tap **Collections**.

- **Create a collection**: From your Collections page, tap the **Add** ⊕ icon. Enter the Collection name, then tap **Create**. You're then prompted to pick a title to add to your Collections. Mark the checkboxes for the titles you want to include in the Collection, then tap **Add**.

- **Add to a collection**: Tap and hold a title, then tap **Add to Collection**. Mark the checkbox beside each Collection you want to add the item to. Tap **Add**.

- **Edit your collection**: Go to a **Collections** library, then tap the collection you want to edit.

  1. To change the name of a collection, tap the title of the Collection, type the Collection name into the field, then tap **Done**.

  2. To remove an item from a Collection, press and hold the item, then move it outside the Collection.

  3. **To add an item to the collection**: Tap the **Add** ⊕ icon, tap the checkbox next to each title you want to include in the Collection, then tap **Add**.

  4. **Delete a collection**: Press and hold the collection, then tap **Delete Collection**.

Book Lovers, Rejoice: Free Kindle Books!

Kindle Buffet is a daily website that features a hand-picked list of great Kindle books being offered free that day. Includes mysteries, romance, science-fiction, horror, non-fiction and more. Today's best-sellers and yesterday's classics. You may never need to pay for a book again! See for yourself by visiting

www.KindleBuffet.com

Allison (A Kane Novel)

Mystery, Thriller & Suspense
Author: Steve Gannon

Allison Kane, a journalism student at UCLA, takes a summer job as a TV news intern—soon becoming involved in a scandalous murder investigation and the media firestorm that follows—a position that pits her squarely against her iron-fisted police detective father.

Cafenova (Clairmont Series)

Christian Fiction > Romance
Author: S. Jane Scheyder

Leaving her broken heart behind in Seattle, Maddy Jacobs starts a new life on the coast of Maine. Although running a Bed and Breakfast has always been her dream, restoring the sprawling Victorian inn is a massive undertaking. Her contractor, competent, handsome, and built like a Greek god, could be the answer to her prayers. If she can keep her wits about her, she might just survive the summer.

20 Things I've Learned as an Entrepreneur

Small Business & Entrepreneurship
Author: Alicia Morga

20 Things I've Learned as an Entrepreneur is the summary of lessons leading female technology entrepreneur Alicia Morga learned as a first-time entrepreneur in Silicon Valley. If you're an entrepreneur or if you've only dreamed about starting your own business, this quick important read is for you.

4 ► MUSIC TO YOUR EARS

We've talked about video, we've talked about print, and now we're talking about music. Yes, the Kindle Fire is a multimedia machine. When it comes to digital music, your options are wide open. You can buy it from Amazon and load it right on your device or stream it from the Cloud to save storage space on your device. You can load your existing music collection, including copies of any of your old CDs you've "burned." And you can purchase more music through Apple's iTunes Store and other providers.

Your Kindle Fire plays MP3 files, the most common format for digital music. And the Fire has some great features to enhance your listening pleasure, like automatically finding missing album artwork.

Above: Browsing the Music Library and Store

Buy and Download Music

You can shop for and download music from Amazon's MP3 store using your Kindle Fire if you're in the United States. Remember, your music files are stored in Amazon's Cloud Player for free, and the ones you've purchased from Amazon don't count against the regular 5-GB storage limit. Music is available for playback or download to any Kindle Fire, computer or compatible mobile device. To shop for new tunes:

1. From your **Home** screen, tap **Music**, then tap **Store**.

2. Find some music you'd like to buy by using the search box. You can also browse categories like **Best Sellers** by swiping from the left of your screen.

3. Tap the button displaying the price. Confirm your purchase by tapping **Buy**—or if the song or album is offered free, tap **Get**. To listen to a sample, tap **Play** beside the song title.

4. To go to your library, from the **Home** screen, tap **Music**. Swipe from the left edge of your screen to see categories such as **Playlists, Artists, Albums, Songs**, or **Genres**. Tap a song or album to open it. After the download is complete, you can listen.

Listen To Music

To listen to a song or album, tap **Music** from your **Home** screen. Tap the song or album to open it, and use these playback controls:

⏮ Go to the previous track.

⏭ Go to the next track.

▶ Resume playback.

⏸ Pause the song.

🔁 Tap once to repeat all songs in the album or playlist. Tap twice to repeat the current song indefinitely.

🔀 Shuffle all songs in an album or playlist.

🔊 Adjust the volume. (Or use the volume buttons on the back of your Kindle Fire.)

➕ Create a playlist. Enter the name of the playlist and tap **Save**. Add more music to the playlist by pressing and holding an album or song and tap **Add** to **Playlist**.

ⓘ Visit the Amazon MP3 store to learn about the artist and find more music.

Import Music to the Cloud

If you already have some music stored on your computer, you can import up to 250 songs to Amazon's Cloud Player for free. Cloud Player premium subscribers can import up to 250,000 songs. Amazon provides free software to locate your music in programs like iTunes or Windows Media Player and import it into your Amazon account. Visit http://bit.ly/ImportMusic

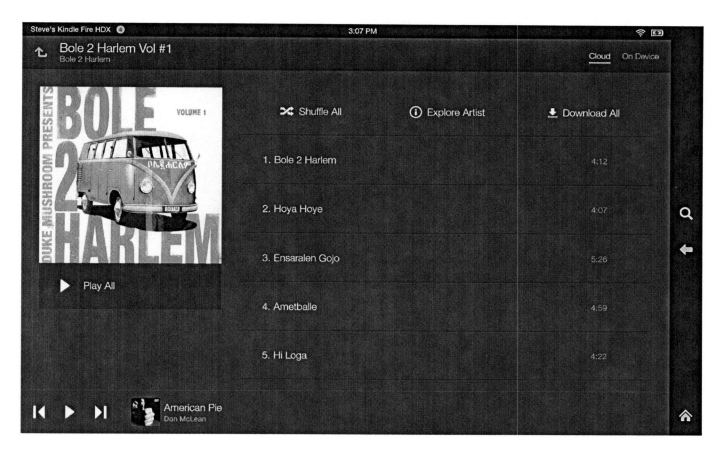

Above: An album stored in the Cloud, viewing the track listing

View Music Lyrics With X-Ray for Music

Your Kindle fire can display the lyrics for songs while you listen using the **X-Ray for Music** feature. If it's available for a particular song, you'll see **[+Lyrics]** next to the song in your music library.

- **View X-Ray** – From the **Now Playing** screen, press and drag the **X-Ray Lyrics** box upward. Or rotate your Kindle to landscape mode.

- **Scroll through lyrics** – Swipe up or down through the lyrics.

- **Jump to a different section of the song** – Tap any line in the lyrics to go to that part of the song.

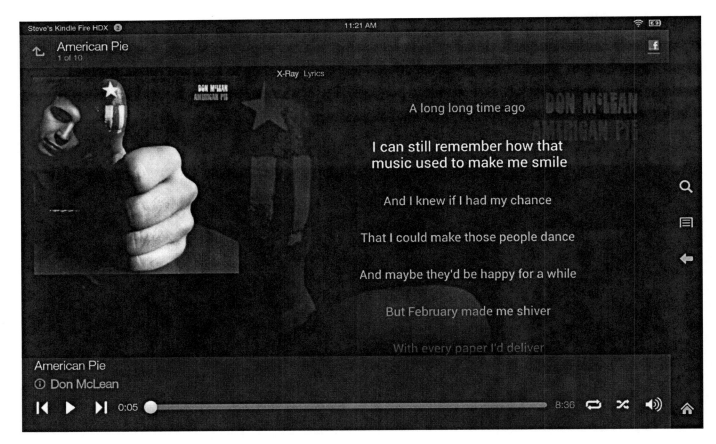

Above: Displaying song lyrics using X-Ray for Music

Uploading Audio Files to the Cloud

Amazon's Cloud provides an alternate means of storing your music. The basic plan gives you 5 GB of storage for your music collection, and you can upgrade to an unlimited storage plan if necessary.

To upload music to the Cloud, you'll need to download the "Amazon MP3 Uploader," a free application that locates music files on your computer and copies them to the Cloud. The uploader is compatible with MP3 files and ACC files, which you may have if you're an iTunes user.

1. Visit www.amazon.com/cloudplayer to access the music you have stored on the Amazon Cloud.

2. Click on "**Upload your music.**" If you already have the MP3 Uploader installed, you'll be taken to the application. If not, you'll be prompted to download the software.

3. Install the application and it will begin searching your computer for audio files. If you want to handle the search manually, click the option on the prompt and you'll be presented with the option to browse manually.

TIP: If you have a very large music collection and don't want to wait for the entire collection to upload, transfer the albums you want to upload to a separate directory on your computer. Then you can browse that directory manually.

Transfer Music From Your Computer to Your Kindle

Perhaps you already have a collection of music files on your computer. You can transfer that music from your computer to your Kindle Fire with the micro-USB cable that came with your Kindle.

When you connect your Kindle Fire to a Windows computer, your device appears as a storage drive as in the illustration below. This enables you to "sideload" the music directly from your computer's hard drive.

1. From your computer, locate the music you want to transfer from your computer to your Kindle Fire.

2. Connect your Kindle Fire to your computer with the micro-USB cable. (On a Windows computer, your Kindle Fire will appear in the **My Computer** folder; on a Mac, the Kindle will appear on your desktop.)

3. Open the Kindle Fire folder (titled Kindle) on your computer, and then open the **Internal storage** folder.

4. Open your Kindle's **Music** folder. Copy your files.

5 ► ENJOY MOVIES AND TV SHOWS

Along with its great picture quality, the Kindle Fire provides access to Amazon's vast library of downloadable and streaming content. The video department is, for many Kindle Fire users, the most exciting of all. Your Kindle Fire purchase comes with a free one-month trial of Amazon Prime, giving you access to a huge library of movies that you can watch for free. You can also choose to pay for movies or television shows that aren't part of the Amazon Prime deal. There are literally thousands of movies that you can choose from on this service.

Once you've purchased a video, it will appear in your video library, or if you choose to watch it from the Amazon servers, it will begin streaming immediately.

When you choose to purchase an Amazon Prime eligible movie, you'll be presented with the option to stream it or buy it, along with additional purchase options.

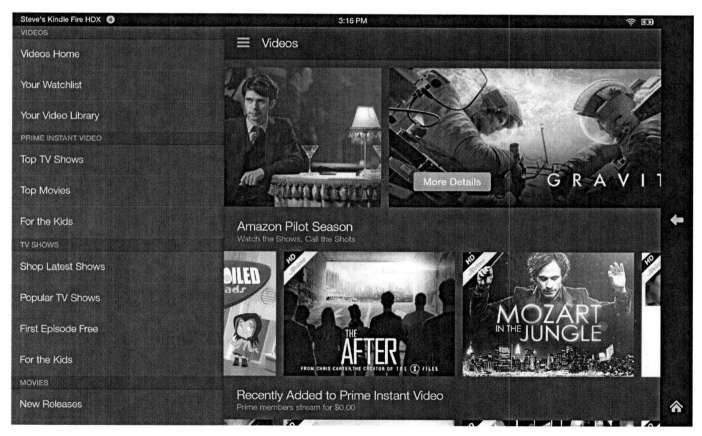

Above: Browsing the Kindle Fire's video content library and store

Buy or Rent Movies and TV shows

Amazon's **Instant Video** service enables you to watch digital movies and TV shows on your Kindle Fire or other compatible TV or streaming device. The store offers videos for rental or purchase. With an Amazon Prime membership, you'll also have access to a huge catalog of videos you can watch at no additional cost.

1. To visit the Instant Video store, from your Kindle's **Home** screen, tap **Videos**.

2. Locate videos you want to buy or rent by using the **Search** box. Narrow your search by swiping from the left edge of the screen to browse categories like **Top Movies**.

3. Tap **Rent** or **Buy** on the video detail page.

Amazon Instant Video is available only to U.S. customers.

Briefly: Two Ways of Buying Streaming Video

Amazon provides two options for buying streaming video: You can purchase it outright, or you can rent it. If you purchase a video, you're free to stream it whenever you want from any compatible device—now, and any time in the future. You can download the video to any compatible device to watch it at your leisure when you're offline—but it may only be stored on two devices at once. On the other hand, if you choose to rent a video, you'll have only 24 hours to finish watching it.

Videos offered free through Amazon Prime are handled differently. With a Prime membership, you can stream these videos whenever you want and however many times you want. You cannot, however, download them for storage on your device.

Videos that you download to your Kindle will appear in your Library, just as is the case with other media.

TIP: If you have young children in your home, it's best to supervise their use of video on the Kindle. If 1-Click purchasing is enabled—and your Kindle has no Parental Controls enabled—children can run up quite a tab without understanding the cost of video purchases.

Explore Movies and TV Shows With X-Ray

You can discover details and trivia about actors, characters and music in video scenes using X-Ray.

- **View the X-Ray panel** – Begin playing a movie or TV show with **X-Ray** enabled. X-Ray cards will appear in the panel, identifying the actors or characters as they appear on the screen, background music or trivia.

- **View information about the movie or TV show** – Tap a card in the X-Ray panel to pause playback, then tap **Actors**, **Characters**, **Trivia** or **Music** to view expanded information.

Above: Learn more about actors and characters in a scene with X-Ray.

Mirror Your Screen on Your HDTV or Media Streaming Device

If you want a big-screen experience from your Kindle video, you can wirelessly fling—or "mirror"—your Kindle content on a compatible HDTV or media streaming device (like a Roku set-top box or a PlayStation 3 game console). First you'll need to turn on your TV or streaming device so it's "discoverable," so your Kindle Fire can identify it and connect wirelessly. Review the instructions for this in the manual included with your TV or streaming device.

1) Swipe down from the top of your Kindle Fire's screen to access **Quick Settings**, then tap **Settings**.

2) Tap **Display & Sounds**, then tap **Display Mirroring**. Your Kindle will search for compatible devices within range.

3) Next to your device, tap **Connect**. The first connection may take 10 to 20 seconds. If your device successfully connects, you'll see the word **Mirroring** under your device name. Tap **Stop Mirroring** to end the connection.

Using the 'Second Screen' for Video Streaming

If your TV or steaming device isn't compatible for mirroring, you might be able to use an HDMI display dongle, an adapter you connect to your TV or streaming device. Another option is to use the **Second Screen** feature, a brand new feature for the Kindle Fire HDX. For the latest information on this feature and compatible devices, visit: http://bit.ly/KindleMediaStreaming

Streaming Video Versus Downloading Video

"Streamed" video is simply video which is stored remotely and not on your personal device or Cloud account. If you've ever watched YouTube or accessed the Netflix online service, you're familiar with streaming, which is highly dependent on your Internet connection.

By contrast, "local" video files are stored directly on your device. You can download them via Wi-Fi or load them from your computer using the USB cable. Once stored on your device, they can be accessed without an Internet connection.

Streaming and local video have advantages and disadvantages:

Streaming Pros

- No local storage space required

- No downloading time required

- Wide availability

- You can easily abandon the video and you don't have to delete the file

- Streaming services offer good selection and economy through Amazon Prime or outside services such as Netflix

Streaming Cons

- Strong, continuous Wi-Fi connection is required

- Playback may be interrupted by network issues

- Video may not be available after a time

- Selection is more limited compared to downloaded options

Local Pros

- Stutter-free playback

- Fast loading, no delays or buffering

- Video quality may be superior to streaming services

- You own the video and can archive it on your computer

Local Cons

- Consumes lots of storage space

- Requires outright purchase, which can be more expensive

- If you lose your devices where your local video is stored, you've permanently lost the content

- Self-loaded videos—transferred from your computer— do not appear in your Kindle Fire's **Video** library

6 ► FIND FUN AND EDUCATIONAL APPS

With the potential to download apps created by thousands of Android developers, your Kindle Fire's horizons are virtually unlimited. The availability of thousands of apps takes the Kindle Fire to another level beyond its out-of-the-box functionality.

Just as with the other sections of your Kindle Fire Home screen, there is a **Store** button that enables you to shop via Amazon. You'll also be able to download one paid application for free on a daily basis at the App Store home page. You can access Amazon's App Store from your device, or on the web at www.amazon.com/mobile-apps/b?node=2350149011

TIP: The customer ratings on apps in the Amazon App Store are a good indication of their quality. Be sure to scan the reviews before investing time or money with an app.

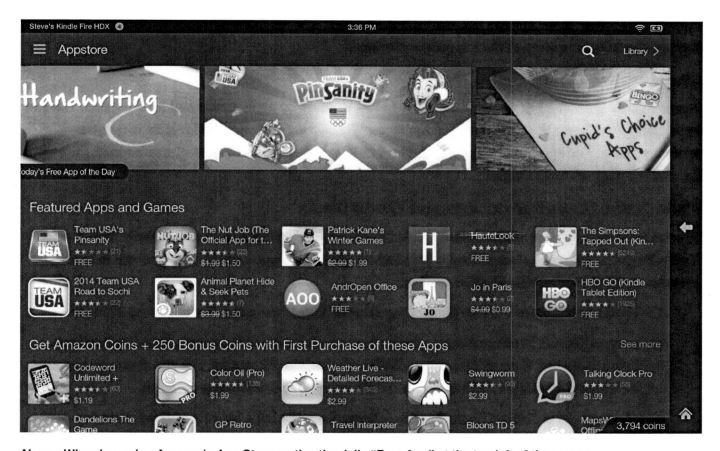

Above: When browsing Amazon's App Store, notice the daily "Free App" at the top left of the screen.

Buy and Download Apps and Games

You can search for and purchase games and mobile apps in the **Amazon Appstore for Android**.

1. From **Home**, tap **Apps** or **Games**, then tap **Store**.

2. Locate the app or game you'd like to buy.

   (a) In the **Search** box, enter some text and tap the magnifying glass.

   (b) Narrow your search by swiping from the left edge of the screen to browse categories such as **New Releases**.

3) To purchase, tap the button displaying the price (or tap **FREE** if it's a free app or game), then tap **Get App**. If you're purchasing a paid app or game, complete the purchase using 1-Click payment or Amazon Coins. The app or game automatically downloads and installs.

4) Tap **Open** to view the app or game.

Amazon's App Store is divided into categories: Games, Entertainment, Productivity, and so forth. Take a look through the available apps and you'll find an incredible range of products that allow you to use your Kindle in novel ways. The selection ranges from games to office suites and beyond.

TIP: Even though many apps are free, you still need to have "1-Click Payment" enabled at Amazon in order to "purchase" them. Ensure you have a default credit card established with your Amazon account so that you can take advantage of the many free offerings.

Use Amazon Coins

Amazon Coins is a virtual currency you can use to buy Kindle Fire apps, games and in-app items. You can buy a Coins bundle at a discount from the Appstore. You also earn promotional credits when you purchase Kindle Fire apps and in-app items. For more details, click the **How do I use coins?** Link on the product page of eligible items.

View Game Statistics on Amazon GameCircle

You can view and compare achievements, leaderboards and time played in a game directly from your Kindle Fire with **Amazon GameCircle**. This feature syncs your game statistics so you can resume your progress on other GameCircle-enabled devices.

1) **Find your games** – From **Home**, tap **Games** in the navigation bar at the top of the screen.

2) **Access GameCircle settings** – Swipe from the left edge of the screen, then tap **Settings**. Select **Amazon GameCircle** from the list of apps. On this screen, you can choose to show or hide your GameCircle nickname or turn **Whispersync for Games** on or off.

3) **Manage your GameCircle Profile** – Swipe from the left edge of the screen, then tap **Profile**. Tap **Edit** to change your GameCircle nickname and avatar.

4) **View time-played, leaderboard scores and achievements** – Press and hold a game in your Library, then tap **Summary**.

To add friends to GameCircle:

1) From the **Games** library: From **Home**, tap **Games**, swipe from the left edge of the screen, tap **Friends**, then tap **Add Friends**. Enter a nickname to find a GameCircle friend.

2) From the Game Summary page: Tap a user's avatar to visit their profile, then tap **Friend**.

Recommended Apps

Plenty of great apps can be loaded onto your Kindle Fire that provide different types of entertainment and to customize the look and feel of your device. The following are a few examples of excellent apps that will help you get the most from your Kindle Fire.

XiiaLive – Internet Radio

No matter how much great music you have stored on your device or available in the Cloud, occasionally you'd rather hear something fresh and new. Streaming Internet music provides relief. For example, Internet radio stations broadcast online, offering an incredible variety of music in every genre. If you want someone else do the work of selecting the tunes, streaming radio is a great option and that brings us to our first app, **XiiaLive**, which is free. There's also a "Pro" version with more features and no advertising.

XiiaLive allows you to play Internet streams in most formats, and you can open them directly from your browser when you find the web page they're hosted on.

To find and download this app, search the **App Store** for "XiiaLive."

Angry Birds Free

You've surely heard the name. **Angry Birds** is a game that allows you to enjoy some classic, addicting arcade-style gaming on your Kindle Fire. It's free, and you can download it instantly from the Amazon App Store. Kids of all ages enjoy this one, and it can make long road trips more tolerable.

TIP: Many apps, Angry Birds included, have a free version that contains advertising, and a paid version without ads. If you really love the free version, it's hard to resist buying the paid version for a few dollars more. But this free/paid system enables you to sample almost everything without risking a dime.

Utilities Apps

Some of the utilities available for the Kindle Fire keep you safe and make it easier to get the most out of it. Here are a few to consider.

Wi-Fi Analyzer

The Kindle Fire needs a Wi-Fi to connect to the Internet, and sometimes, you need a bit more information than the Settings panel gives you. This is where **Wi-Fi Analyzer Free** really shines. It gives you a great deal of information on the wireless networks around you, including a meter that shows you their strength. This makes it a lot easier to find the sweet spots in some buildings where the Wi-Fi might work better than in others. It also allows you to see how many networks are in your area and whether or not yours may be on a channel that is too crowded.

Imo Free Video Calls and Text

The **imo** app allows you to connect to multiple types of instant-messaging services and place video phone calls. This app is a great choice for anyone who uses these services for work or pleasure.

The imo app is compatible with: AIM, Facebook Chat, Google Talk, ICQ, Jabber, MSN, MySpace Chat, Skype and Yahoo.

Sometimes, the best thing about a Kindle Fire is that it lets you get away from your desktop computer and still enjoy everything the Internet has to offer. With imo, you can be sure that you don't miss any important messages when you get away from your desk for a while!

Productivity Apps

Kingsoft Office for Android

The **Kingsoft** app allows you to open and edit documents in the most popular office formats, including Microsoft. It's a required equipment if you plan on using your Kindle Fire as a productivity tool.

Tap the icon and accept the license agreement. If you want the pro version of this software, you can purchase it from the Amazon App Store. It's one of the handiest utilities to have on your Kindle Fire.

Evernote

Evernote is an application that allows you to write notes, take picture notes, record audio notes, clip web pages, and much more. If you do research in any capacity—for fun or business—it's a must. You can share your notes between your devices, so whatever you clip on your PC or Mac will be available on your Kindle Fire.

Office Calculator Free

The **Office Calculator Free** program is a great choice for anyone who wants more advanced capabilities out of their calculator but doesn't venture into trigonometry or other advanced forms of math. As the name says, if you need an office calculator, this one might be for you. It even keeps a tape of your calculations! The free version has small advertisements at the top of the screen, while the paid version does not.

Managing Apps

Apps consume storage space on your device. So if you install an app and you don't like it, remember to uninstall it to free up that space. You don't want your Kindle stuffed with apps you don't use.

To check your App storage quickly:

1. Swipe downward from the top of the screen to open **Quick Settings**, then tap **Settings**.

2. Tap **Device**

3. Look for "**Storage.**" You'll see a graphical representation of how much of your storage space is consumed by the various types of content.

Deleting Apps

Removing apps can be done in two different ways. The first simply removes the App from your device, but leaves it in the Amazon Cloud so it's available for downloading again later. Considering the amount of storage you get with the Amazon Cloud—and the small size of most apps—this is a sensible option.

To remove an App and leave it in the Amazon Cloud:

1. On your home-screen, click **Apps**.

2. Click **On Device** on top of the App Library.

3. Press and hold the icon for the App you want to remove.

4. Select **Remove from Device** from the pop-up menu.

This will send the App back into the Amazon Cloud, freeing up space on your device. Note that some apps come pre-installed on the Kindle Fire, and these can't be removed. You can remove them from your Favorites, which means they won't appear in your library, but they remain on your device. The good news: most of these default apps are merely Internet shortcuts, such as IMDb, so they consume very little storage space.

To Permanently Delete an App

If you want to delete an App permanently, you'll have to do so from the **Your Account** web page at Amazon at https://www.amazon.com/gp/css/homepage.html

1. Under **Digital Content**, click **Your Apps and Devices**.

2. On the left side of the screen, in the **Your Kindle Library** section, click **Your Apps**.

3. Scan the list of apps to find the app you want to delete.

4. From the **Actions** drop-down menu, select **Delete this App**.

TIP: Once you delete an App entirely in the manner just described, it's gone for good. If you want to reinstall it on your Kindle, you must purchase it again. Remember, you have plenty of room for storage in the Amazon Cloud. Even if you've tired of an application, keep it in the Cloud if there's a chance you might use it again.

To Open the Built-in Clock App:

From Home, tap **Apps**, then tap **Clock**.

To add or remove a clock:

- Tap + , then select a city from the list or type the name of the city you wish to add. To remove a clock, press and hold the city, then tap **Remove**.

To set an alarm, swipe from the left edge of the screen, then tap **Alarms**. Tap + to add a new alarm. Select the time, schedule and alarm sound, then tap **Set Alarm**.

To set a time, swipe from the left edge of the screen, then tap **Timer**. Set the timer, then tap **Start**. When the timer completes, your Kindle will beep until you double-tap the screen.

While the timer is running, you can add additional time, pause it, or clear the time by using the on-screen controls.

To use a stopwatch, swipe from the left edge of the screen, tap **Stopwatch**, and tap the **Start** icon ▶.

Nightstand Mode resembles a clock radio with a soft red display. Swipe from the left edge of the screen, then tap **Nightstand**.

7 ► FEED YOUR KINDLE WITH FREE CONTENT

After all that discussion about apps, videos, pictures and web browsing, it might be easy to forget that the Kindle Fire is, first and foremost, an e-reader. Not all e-readers can handle the same formats and Kindle devices are no exception.

Amazon benefits mightily from consumer loyalty. By linking their device so strongly to the AZW and MOBI formats they use, they make the average user assume they can only read e-books that are bought directly from Amazon. Fortunately, you actually can read any e-book format you want, thanks to a great program called Calibre, a program that runs on Windows or Mac desktop computers. Calibre can find all sorts of valuable non-Amazon content and format it and deliver it to your Kindle.

Calibre is free, it's stable and, to put it in the most direct terms, it's awesome—it can deliver you hundreds of dollars' worth of newspaper, magazine and book content every day, 365 days a year. The only challenge is finding the time to read that gusher of great content you're piping to your Kindle.

Using Calibre With the Kindle Fire e-Book Reader

Let's jump right in and download the Calibre application to your computer. I have been using the program, along with thousands of others, for the past three years. The best things in life are free, and believe me, Calibre is one of them.

1. Go to www.calibre-ebook.com and select "Download Calibre."

2. Open the downloaded program to install the package once it's completed.

On your first run, you'll get the **Welcome Wizard**. This is designed to help you set up your libraries and to import your books, as well as to help you select the correct device!

The first screen will set your **Calibre Library** directory. The default choice is a good one. On the next screen, you'll have to choose your device. Obviously, choose Kindle Fire.

This sets the program up so that it knows to look for your Kindle Fire when you click the **Send to Device** icon.

When you have the program installed, launch it, and study the interface for a moment. This program is capable of doing many things; even offering you a way to shop for content across a number of different stores. What we'll concern ourselves with first, however, is opening up new sources of literature by using the features built into this program that allow you to convert books from other formats into ones that your Amazon Kindle can read.

All the News You Can Eat, and Calibre Picks Up the Check

OK, I'll admit it. I'm a book nut. But I have an even bigger problem. I'm addicted to newspapers, too. I was a "news junkie" before anyone ever heard of such a thing. Twenty-five years ago, I paid about $75 a month to have three different newspapers dropped at my doorstep every morning—my local paper, the *Wall Street Journal*, and the *New York Times*.

Now, since I discovered Calibre, I've been reading six newspapers a day—plus bunch of blogs and magazines like *Newsweek* and *Time*—and it doesn't cost me one red cent. The *Washington Post*. The *New York Post*. And, if I still have time, I can read the *Onion* and a couple others—just to get my humor fix. Your local newspaper is probably available, too. Calibre downloads the content they post on their websites, and sends it, nicely formatted, to your Kindle. The only cost is the few minutes you'll spend setting it up once, and then it works every day. Here how to get started:

1. Click on **Fetch News** in the Menu.

2. Select your language.

3. Select a news source.

In the next illustration, you can see that I've selected the *Washington Post*.

Note that I've opted to have it download automatically every day of the week after 6am. If you were the ultimate news junkie, you could set it to download the Associated Press news wire every 10 minutes.

Calibre has hundreds of different news sources available in a huge number of languages, you just click them and enjoy—free.

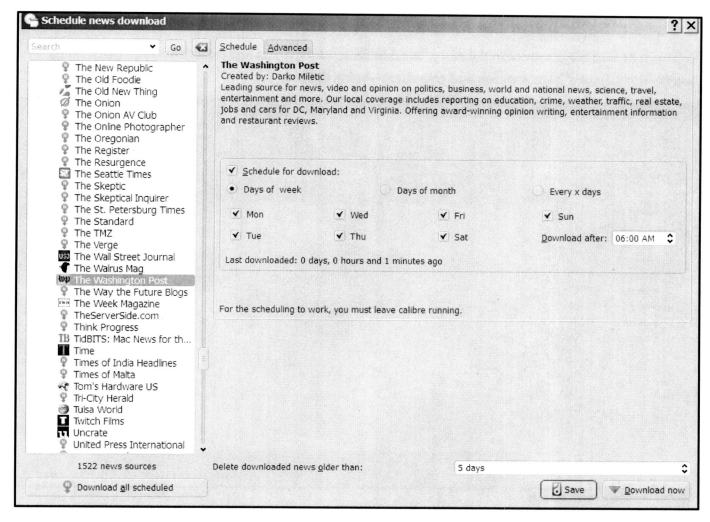

Above: Selecting the *Washington Post* news download.

Of course, you have to leave Calibre running so it automatically downloads your news sources. If you have several news sites on your list, it will take a while. Personally, I leave my computer on 24/7, and Calibre is finding news for me constantly, and feeding my Kindle. In the old days, I used to finish my three newspapers and still want more. Now, with Calibre, I don't have a prayer of skimming everything I'm tempted to read every day.

TIP: In this section, we're talking about downloading content for free. It sounds too good to be true, but it's totally above board. We're not stealing, we're just using the stuff that publishers are posting to their websites. Calibre simply does the work of formatting it for the Kindle and emailing it to us.

After the news site has converted, you'll be able to transfer it to your Kindle Fire using the same interface that you use to transfer books. One of the best things about the Calibre program is that it's smart in meaningful ways. The program, for instance, will transfer newspapers to your Newsstand.

E-Books, Calibre and the Kindle

Believe it or not, there's more to the story. In addition to newspapers and magazines, you can manage e-books—downloaded from Amazon and elsewhere—using Calibre.

Above: Calibre's main screen

In the illustration above, I haven't added my e-books to the collection yet, so the middle of the screen is blank. There are many ways you can add books to your library. By default, they're sent to the **Calibre Library** folder.

The **Add Books** icon appears at the upper left. Select it, and you'll see the options shown below.

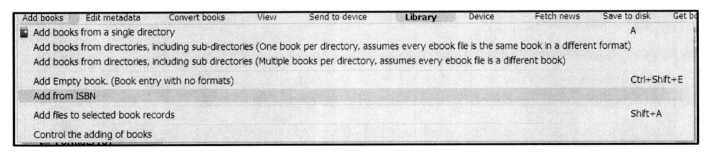

Above: The Add Books dialog

There are quite a few options here, but we'll concentrate adding one book to the library in a format that Kindle just doesn't like.

In this case, I'm going to add a book that's stored in the EPUB format—a popular one on many sites—that I want to read on my Amazon Kindle Fire in the native Kindle AZW or MOBI format.

To start, click on **Add books from a single directory** and browse to the directory that you want. In the illustration below, I've chosen the book "pg1062.epub" which is actually *The Raven* by Edgar Allen Poe, which I have in the EPUB format that the Kindle will not read. I downloaded it from Project Gutenberg, a site that has plenty of public domain eBooks to choose from.

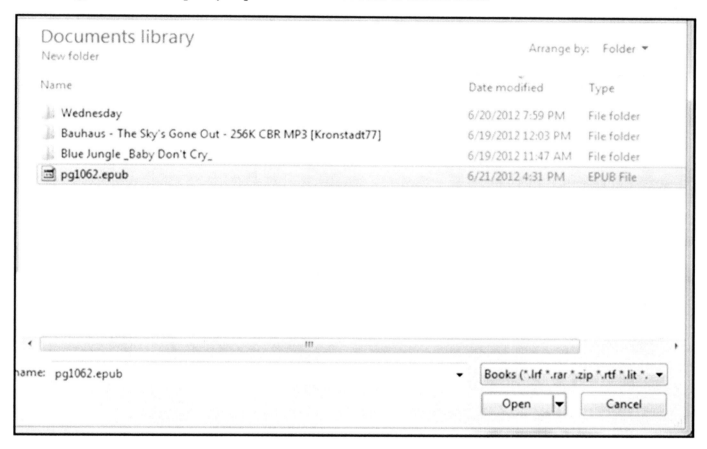

Above: Choosing a book to import

In the illustration below, you can see that the book has been added to my **Calibre Library**. Notice that even the cover art came over with the import, as did the description and other metatag information. This is one of the handiest features with the Calibre program. I'll change it to more suitable cover art and change the metatags during the conversion process so that they're more descriptive and accurate.

Above: The e-book from Project Gutenberg now appears in My Library.

Before I dump this to my Kindle Fire, I have to convert it. Fortunately, Calibre makes that very easy to do.

Highlight the title and select the **Convert Books** icon and then select **Convert individually**. The screen pictured below appears.Take a look at the options available. The **Metadata** selection controls the description, publisher credit, and other information associated with the book. Be sure to fill these out if they're not filled out already. They're important organizational tools.

Above: The Convert screen

You can also change the cover image, which I've done using a public domain cover that I downloaded. I could technically use any image I wanted, however, as long as it doesn't violate anyone's copyright. You can change the **Look and Feel** of the output, which alters the text formatting, and more. One thing that Calibre does very well is give you options!

Because this book needs to be readable on the Kindle Fire, we'll go with the MOBI format, which you can see in the upper right-most dropdown list.

TIP: You can convert more than one file at once, but it takes a lot of time. If you're going to do so, you might want to get a cup of coffee, order a pizza, or do something else to pass the time. If you have a slow computer, consider making your own pizza from scratch!

Now, the file has been converted to the MOBI format, which the Kindle Fire will be entirely happy with, but we have to move it over to the Kindle Fire device, of course.

Select, **Send to Device** from the top menu on the main screen. It will pick the device that you set up during the **Welcome Wizard**. Because the Kindle Fire doesn't take an SD card, you can just choose

Send to main memory from the dropdown list. If you did have a device with additional onboard storage, Calibre would give you the option to send it to that storage.

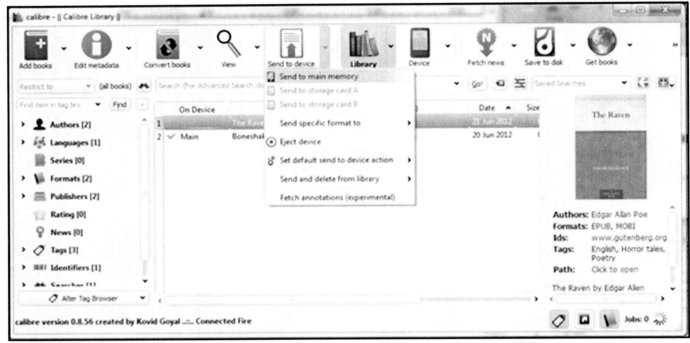

Above: Sending the book to the Kindle.

When the book has been sent, you'll see the listing for it under the **On Device** heading change. If I go to my Books library on my Kindle Fire and look under the titles available on my device, it shows right up.

This is only one of the functions that Calibre offers you. It's an amazingly powerful program. We'll explore it more, but be aware that this is going to be one of your most important resources for getting free books off of the Internet. The sites that offer works from the public domain sometime don't have them in a format that the Kindle reads. In the future, of course, a format may come along that is incompatible with your Kindle books. Instead of having to buy them in a new format, you'll just be able to convert them!

Let's Go Shopping!

The Kindle Fire makes it easy to go shopping at Amazon, and Calibre makes it easy to go shopping everywhere else. Because it can convert e-books to different formats, that means that you can hit Amazon, Barnes & Noble, Borders, Project Gutenberg or any other site out there and purchase and download books without worrying about the format.

Click on the **Get books** icon on the top of the screen. Because I also have Cherie Priest's book *Boneshaker* on my Calibre and Kindle, I'll get the option to **Search this author**, which I'll do.

If I wanted to, however, I could search for any book using the **Search for e-books** option. I found *The Raven* using that search function. The following search dialog will come up. Along the left hand side of the dialog, pictured below, you'll see options for which stores to search.

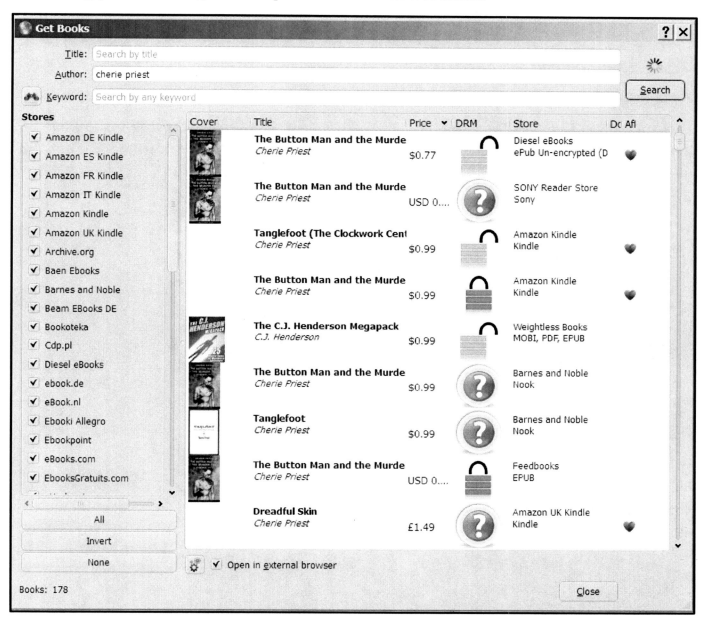

Above: Just part of the Search Results

Notice the locks that appear next to some of the listings. This indicates whether the book has DRM (Digital Rights Management, or copy prevention). This doesn't mean that you cannot move them from device to device, but you need an additional program to do it. It's called Adobe Digital Editions, which is also valuable for downloading books from your public library. Adobe Digital Editions allows you to authorize your e-reader, which allows the publisher to manage the DRM properly.

Clicking on any of the links in the search results will take you to the appropriate page where you can buy the book. This is an amazing feature, when you think about it. Amazon has just about everything in the way of books, of course, but there are always those books that they don't have and you can search other stores to find them if you need to.

The search feature also searches public domain sources for books. Sort the books by price or by DRM status to get to the public domain versions, if one is available.

Kindlefeeder

Another popular third-party Kindle service is Kindlefeeder.com. Like Calibre, it enables you to send content that appears on the Internet to your Kindle via email. I suppose it's a bit easier to use at first, but doesn't have the range of Calibre. See www.kindlefeeder.com

8 ► GET OODLES MORE FREE CONTENT

Finding free content for your Kindle Fire isn't difficult. In fact, you'll find that there are plenty of sites out there—including Amazon itself—offering free content of one type or another. These sites may offer a variety of different types of content, from video to audio to books. While you're exploring them, you'll want to avoid illegal pirate sites.

Now, for the good news: There is actually a ton of free content out there that you can download for your Kindle Fire and, better yet, the majority of it is entirely legal.

Public Domain Books

Many older popular books are no longer under copyright, and so they're in the "Public Domain" and usually available free in e-book formats. For instance, the works of Edgar Allen Poe, Mary Shelly, Jane Austin and Charlotte Bronte were written so long ago, nobody owns the rights anymore. There is a caveat here, however.

Project Gutenberg

search book catalog

- Search Catalog
- Book Categories

search website

- Main Page
- Categories
- News
- Contact Info

donate
Project Gutenberg needs your donation!

Free ebooks - Project Gutenberg

From Project Gutenberg, the first producer of free ebooks.

Book search · Book categories · Browse catalog · Mobile site · Report errors · Terms of use

New Kindle Fire Review

Before you buy: Read our Webmaster's review of the new Kindle Fire.

Some of Our Latest Books

If you buy a specific publisher's edition of a public domain work, that edition is copyrighted. The edition likely has unique material in it that does fall under the copyright protection of the publisher and, therefore, it cannot be reproduced in full. To put it in shorthand terms: You can reproduce *The Raven* all you want, but you cannot reproduce a copyrighted analysis of *The Raven* included in a printing of the poem.

There are several sites that offer public domain books. The most well-known is likely Project Gutenberg, located at www.gutenberg.org

Exploring Project Gutenberg

The illustration above shows the Project Gutenberg homepage. The left navigation menu gives you access to the site's entire book catalog. You can choose to **Search Catalog, Browse Catalog** or you can view **Book Categories**.

Let's search for a well-known suspense story, *The Turn of the Screw* by Henry James. Here is the result from Project Gutenberg:

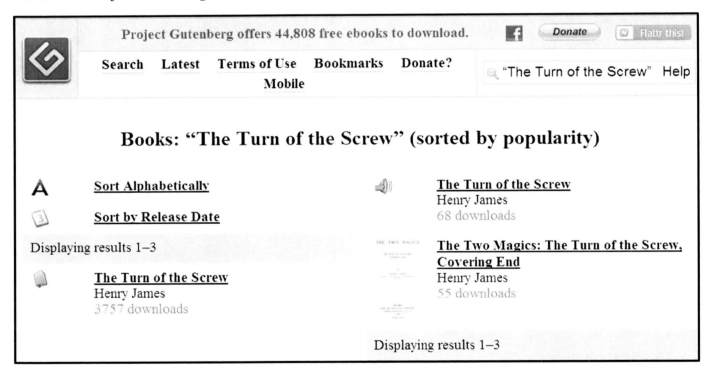

Above: Search results for *Turn of the Screw* at Project Gutenberg.

Notice that, on the right of the page, there are two results listed. The first result is a link to the e-book version. The second result is a link to the audio version of the story. (Project Gutenberg has a lot of audio books that are public domain and that are read by volunteers. If you want to stock up on audio books for a long trip, this is a good place to do it!)

Let's click on the link to the e-book version of *The Turn of the Screw*.

Above: The e-book versions of *The Turn of the Screw*

Project Gutenberg will typically offer books in a variety of formats. Notice that there are HTML, EPUB, Kindle, PLocker, QiOO Mobile and Plain Text versions of this e-book.

Simply click on the link to download the e-book and save it to your computer. You can either transfer the book to your Kindle Fire manually or you can do so through your Calibre library, which will allow you to assign it a cover and other metadata, as I did with *The Raven*.

TIP: Project Gutenberg oftentimes offers books with images or without the images. Since you have the Kindle Fire's color display, you'll definitely want to download the version with images.

Public Domain Books on Amazon

Like Project Gutenberg, Amazon offers thousands of classic Public Domain works absolutely free. These books remain free all year long, and many of them are the same texts available through Project Gutenberg.

Let's do a search for "Bronte" on Amazon.com. This will bring up books by the Bronte sisters. On the right side of the web page, select **Price—Low to High** and the free public domain books will appear.

TIP: Many rare and out-of-print books are now available as e-books from several different sites. If you've been searching for a book that means a lot to you to own—maybe something from your childhood or with similar sentimental value—be sure to check Project Gutenberg and Amazon. It may well be available on one of these sites.

Even though a particular book might be "free," you'll still need a 1-Click payment method at Amazon to download them. You'll get a receipt in your email that will show the purchase but nothing will show up on your credit card or bank statement.

Lend or Borrow Kindle Books

Remember the days when you'd loan your paperback books to friends, and (depending on the friend) rarely see the book again? Well, a great feature of lending books via your Kindle is that all your books will actually be returned—there's no way around it. Loans are capped at 14 days by Amazon's system.

Not all Kindle books are eligible for lending—the publisher has to agree to the program. When you're shopping for Kindle books nowadays, you'll see a notation—whether lending is **enabled** or not—in the **Product Details** of the book's listing on Amazon.

TIP: Remember, you can loan Kindle books to virtually anyone with an email address, regardless of whether they have a Kindle device. They can read the book on a free Kindle reading app on their computer or smartphone. Kindle reading apps are available free for practically every type of computer, smartphone, and other digital gadgets.

You're allowed to lend Kindle books only once per title. During the loan period, you won't have access to the book.

1. Visit the Kindle store and locate the product page for the book.

2. From the product page, click **Loan this book**.

3. Enter the borrower's email address (their regular email address, not a Kindle address) and an optional personal message.

4. Click **Send Now**.

You can also loan Kindle books from the **Manage Your Kindle** page (www.amazon.com/myk). In the **Actions** menu, select **Loan this title**. Borrowers can return loaned books via **Manage Your Kindle**.

Borrow Books From the Kindle Owner's Lending Library

Amazon Prime members can borrow one book per month from the Kindle Owner's Lending Library with no due dates. Not all books are eligible for borrowing.

1. From the **Home** screen, tap **Books**.

2. Swipe from the left side of the screen, then tap **Kindle Lending Library**. You'll see a display of eligible titles.

3. Make your selection, then tap **Borrow for Free**.

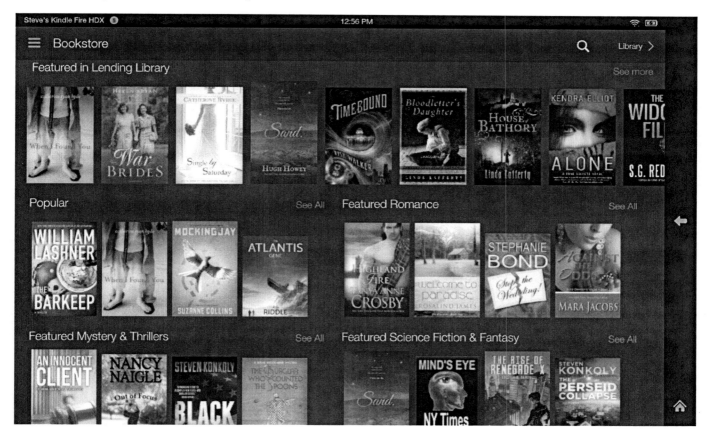

Above: The Kindle Owner's Lending Library.

Borrow Books From a Public Library

You can borrow Kindle books from the websites of local libraries and have them sent to your Kindle or reading app. About 11,000 U.S. libraries offer Kindle books. Just like regular library books, Kindle books may be loaned for a specific period of time. Since only one copy of a Kindle book may be loaned at one time, there might be a waiting period before you can borrow a popular title.

1. Confirm whether your library branch carries Kindle books. Visit your library's website or visit Overdrive, the company that handles library Kindle lending at www.search.overdrive.com

2. Obtain a library card and PIN from your local library.

3. Search for Kindle books at your library's website.

4. At checkout, sign into your Amazon account, and select your Kindle device.

5. Your Kindle should receive the book automatically. If not, sync your device manually.

Amazon sends a courtesy email to remind you three days before the book is due, and another message after the loan period ends. To return the book before the loan period ends, visit **Manage Your Kindle** (www.amazon.com/myk). Click **Actions**, then **Return This Book**.

Finding Free Video

We know there's a ton of free video available through your Amazon Prime account, but what if you want to search beyond Amazon? Fortunately, the Kindle Fire gives you plenty of options in this regard.

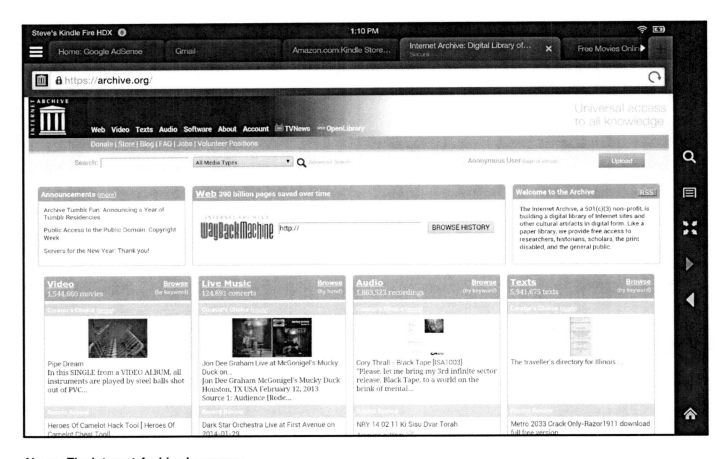

Above: The Internet Archive homepage

Archive.org

Officially known as the Internet Archive, pictured below, Archive.org has a huge collection of Public Domain videos available. The site is free to use. There are government produced clips—the ones from the '50s and '60s being particularly amusing—and there are classic films that have fallen into the public domain. Before you start thinking that all public domain films must be awful, think again! Some of the most well-known and beloved films are in the public domain.

Google Video/YouTube

YouTube.com is one of the best sites for free video of all types. Because much of it is user-generated, you don't have to worry about copyright issues. YouTube is a great place to go if you want to see:

- Viral videos

- Movie trailers

- Classic TV commercials

- Independent news

- Major news organizations' videos

- Much more

Netflix

Even though the Kindle Fire is tied to the Amazon.com webpage, you can still use it to view movies from other sources. If you have a Netflix account, you can watch movies instantly by using the Netflix app available in the Amazon App store. (The app is free but Netflix charges a monthly membership fee.)

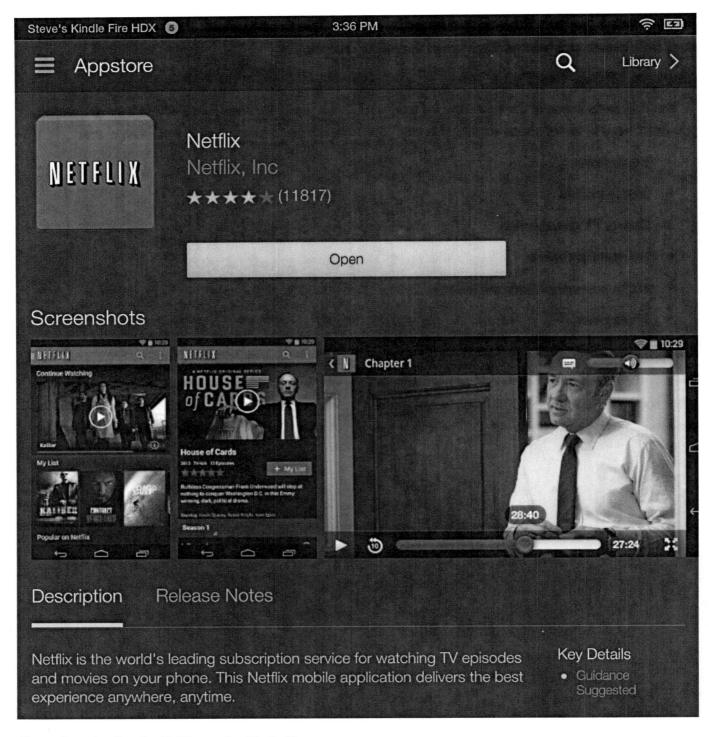

Above: Downloading the Netflix app for Kindle Fire.

Venturing Beyond Amazon's App Store

Amazon's app store has a wide selection of apps, but it's not comprehensive. Not all developers of Android apps publish to the Amazon store. However, these apps are available outside Amazon, and will work just fine on your Kindle Fire. Downloading these non-Amazon apps is sometimes called "sideloading."

A word of caution: Venturing outside Amazon's App Store entails more risk. Some of the apps available outside Amazon are poorly designed, and sometimes these apps contain viruses. The safest place for you to download apps, by far, is the App Store on Amazon. If you want some other options, however, there are alternatives. Several alternative app stores are mentioned below.

If you want to allow the installation of apps from locations outside the Amazon App Store, you'll have to select the appropriate option on your Kindle:

1. Swipe downward from the top of the screen to open **Quick Settings**, then tap **Settings**.

2. Tap **Applications**.

3. Beside **Apps from Unknown Sources**, tap **On**.

This allows you to install applications from any source that you wish. Remember, however, that applications from sources other than Amazon might not be tested or safe.

The next step to going outside Amazon's App Store is to download and install an app called **ES File Explorer**, which is available in Amazon's App Store:

1. From the **Home Screen**, tap **Apps**.

2. On the right side of the top **Navigation Bar**, tap **Store**.

3. Click the **Search icon** 🔍 .

4. Enter the text, **ES File Explorer**, then tap the **Search** icon.

5. Tap the **FREE** icon, then **Get App**. The app installs.

Using the 1Mobile Market App Store

1MobileMarket.com is an Android app marketplace with plenty of great apps that will work with your Amazon Kindle Fire HDX, including many that aren't offered in Amazon's App Store. Many of the apps are free, as you can see in the illustration below. This allows you to break away from Amazon's control of your device. Amazon did a good job with the device, of course, but you paid for a tablet computer and should be able to use it to its fullest! Sometimes apps are barred from Amazon's App Store not because they are inferior, but because they conflict with Amazon's business interests. To give just one example, many e-reader apps are excluded from Amazon's store because they offer a way to obtain reading material without using Amazon's proprietary Kindle format. Amazon, having invested considerably in the Kindle system, understandably wants its customers to stick with the Kindle format as much as possible.

Using your Kindle Fire's web broswer, visit www.1mobile.com , then tap the link for **Market**. You should arrive at http://market.1mobile.com/m/ and see the page illustrated below.

Tap **Download** under the heading **Tablet**.

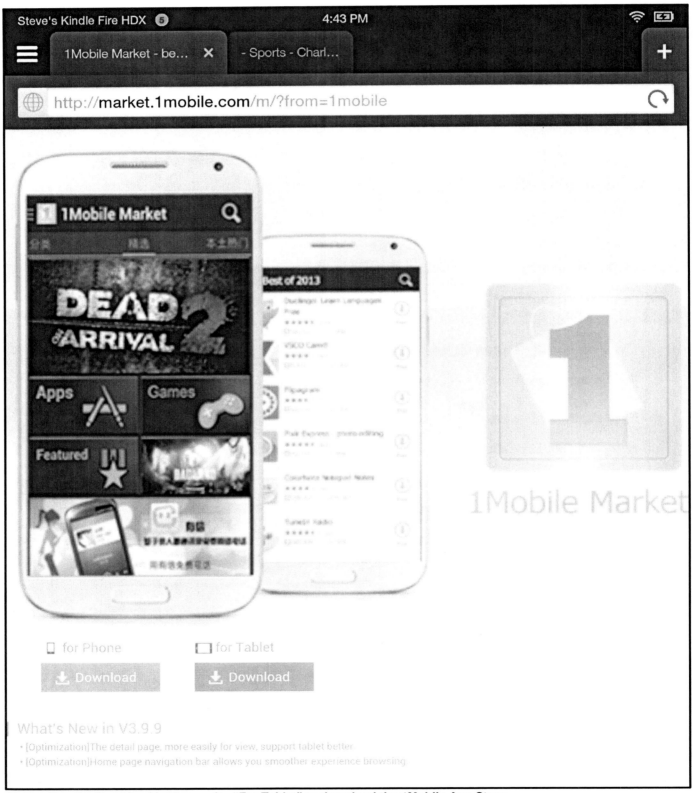

Above: Tap the Download button under "For Tablet" to download the 1Mobile App Store

You'll arrive at the following screen:

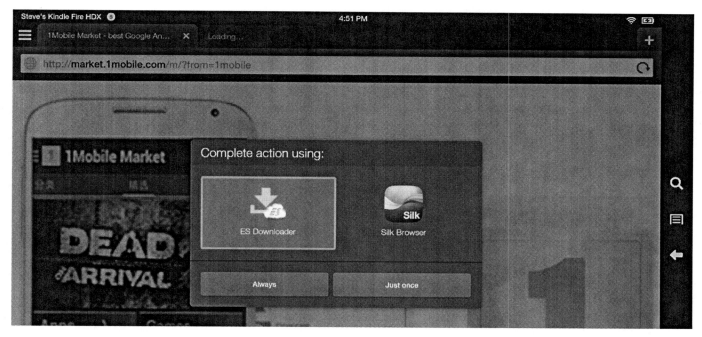

Above: Downloading 1Mobile

As illustrated above, tap **Complete Action** using ES Downloader. The file downloads.

At the next prompt, shown below, tap **Open File**.

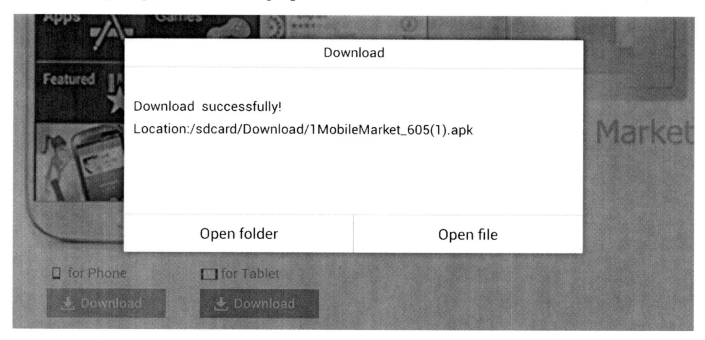

Above: Installing the 1Mobile App Store

On the next screen, shown below, tap **Install** at the bottom.

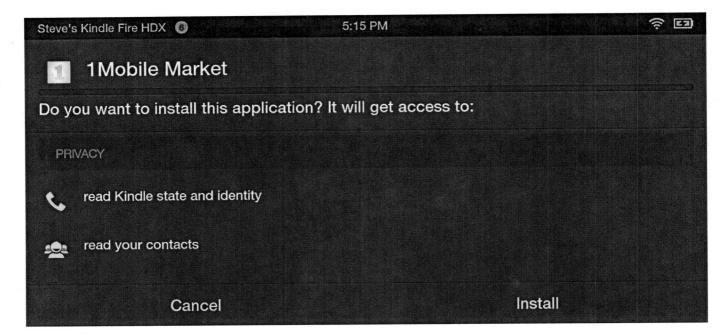

Above: Confirming installation of 1Mobile (illustration is abbreviated)

The app installs. Click **Open** to visit the 1Mobile Market. You can browse apps and download and install them, much like Amazon's store.

Finding Sideloaded Apps

Most sideloaded apps behave nicely, but every once in a while, you'll have difficulty locating a sideloaded app you've already installed. Sometimes they don't appear on the carousel, and won't appear in the Apps Library, either. In that case, you'll need to visit the **Apps Library**, click the **Search** icon at the bottom of the screen, and search for the app by its title.

More Alternative App Stores

Slide ME is another Android app store that offers you more than what you could get at Amazon's app store. See www.slideme.org . They have plenty of games and other free applications that you can choose from. Remember to check the community reviews of applications before you download them; it can prevent you from downloading a dud!

A couple of other alternative app stores:

GetJar – www.getjar.com

Samsung Apps - http://apps.samsung.com

10 ▶ ADVANCED SETTINGS

We've already touched on several of the Kindle Fire's settings options. But just in case, let's do a quick rundown on each setting option. Swipe down from the top of the screen to reveal **Quick Settings**, then tap **Settings**.

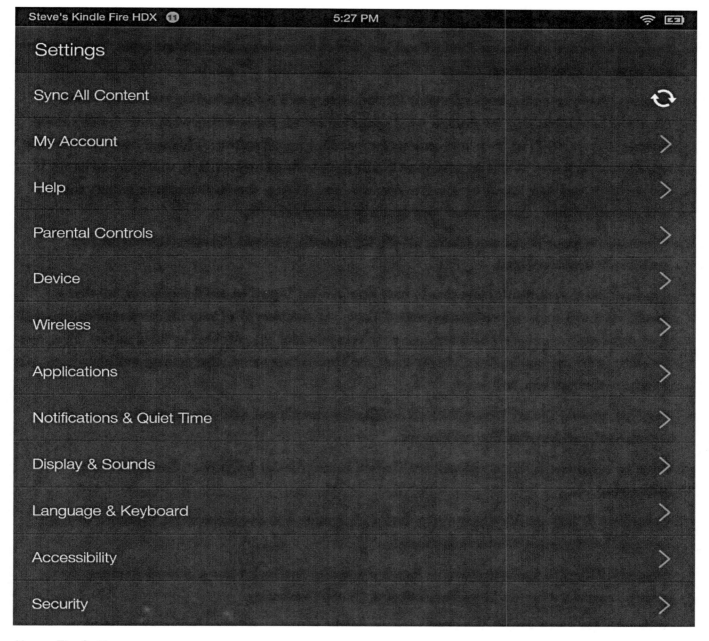

Above: The Settings screen

- **Sync All Content:** Pressing **Sync** causes your Kindle to check to see if everything on your Kindle Fire is synchronized with your Cloud content. If you've just made a purchase and it hasn't appeared on your Kindle, tap this button to sync with the Cloud.

- **My Account:** Here you can switch the Amazon account associated with your Kindle. You can also change your Amazon account name, email address or password, redeem gift cards, and manage your Newsstand subscriptions.

- **Help:** Watch a video demonstrating the **Mayday** technical-support feature. There's also a text user guide for your Kindle Fire.

- **Parental Controls:** Manage Kindle FreeTime, and restrict purchasing, content types, web browsing and access to other features.

- **Device:** The information center for your Kindle. Here, you'll see information such as how much space you have remaining for storage, what operating system you're using, what your device's serial number is, your Wi-Fi address, and options for installing install software obtained outside Amazon's App Store. You'll also be able to reset your Kindle back to its factory settings, which can be handy if you decide to sell your Kindle or give it to someone else. Change the display of your battery charge, view system updates, storage, reset your device to factory defaults.

- **Wireless:** Manage **Airplane Mode**, **Wi-Fi**, **Bluetooth**, **Virtual Private Networks**, and **location-based services**.

- **Applications:** Perhaps this one should have been named "Apps" to avoid confusion, but that's exactly what this menu allows you to control. Here, you can view all of your different applications and their statuses. You can see which ones are running and which are provided by third parties. To access the settings for any applications, simply touch the appropriate name. Also manage audiobooks, music, photos, reader settings, and more.

- **Notifications & Quiet Time:** Mute all notification sounds and hide pop-up notifications. Also, choose how each installed app notifies you.

- **Display & Sounds:** Adjust volume, notification sound, display brightness. Control **Display Mirroring**.

- **Language & Keyboard:** Change your device's language, text-to-speech voice, keyboard language, keyboard settings, and Bluetooth keyboard.

- **Accessibility:** The available **Screen Reader** provides feedback when you touch items on the screen. Control the Screen Magnifier, font size, Closed Captioning.

- **Security:** Set a lock screen password, view credential storage, and view device administrators.

View Notifications and Status Indicators

Notifications and status indicators tell you the status of your device. The Status Bar at the top of the screen shows incoming notifications and displays information about your Kindle Fire. Swipe down from the **Status Bar** at the top of your screen to reveal your notifications, which can include:

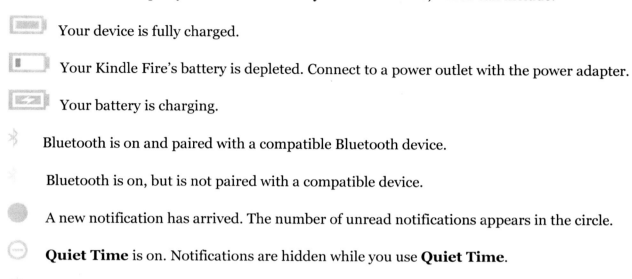

Your device is fully charged.

Your Kindle Fire's battery is depleted. Connect to a power outlet with the power adapter.

Your battery is charging.

Bluetooth is on and paired with a compatible Bluetooth device.

Bluetooth is on, but is not paired with a compatible device.

A new notification has arrived. The number of unread notifications appears in the circle.

Quiet Time is on. Notifications are hidden while you use **Quiet Time**.

You're using an app or website that uses Wi-Fi to estimate your location.

Parental controls are on; access to content and settings is restricted.

Airplane Mode is on. You can't download content, browse the web, or sync your device.

Your Kindle Fire is mirroring its screen on a compatible TV or streaming device.

Your Kindle Fire is connected to a Wi-Fi network with a strong signal.

Your Kindle Fire is connected to a Wi-Fi network with a weak signal.

Your device is connected to a Wi-Fi network but can't connect to the Internet. You might need to enter a password or restart your router and Kindle to establish a connection.

View, Modify or Mute Notifications

To view a notification, swipe down from the top of the screen to access **Quick Settings**. Your notification appears below the Quick Settings menu.

To modify notification settings:

- Press and hold the notification to quickly manage settings for that application.

- Swipe down from the top of the screen to open **Quick Settings**, then tap **Settings**. Tap **Notifications and Quiet Time**, then select an app from the list to allow the app to appear in the notification tray or play a sound when a notification arrives for that app.

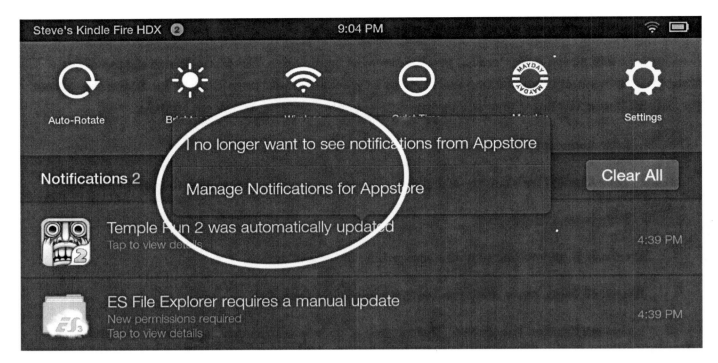

Above: Press and hold notifications to show options for managing them.

Safeguard Your Kindle With Security Settings

If you worry about what would happen if your Kindle were lost or stolen, take note. You can protect the data and personal information on your Kindle Fire by setting up a **Lock Screen Password** or **PIN**.

1. Swipe down from the top of the screen to access **Quick Settings**, then tap **Settings**.

2. Tap **Security**.

3. Beside **Lock Screen Password**, tap **On**. You can create a Simple Numeric PIN, such as four digits, or create a more secure (but time-consuming) password with a combination of letters, numbers, and special characters, making it much more difficult for unauthorized users to access your Kindle Fire.

Forgotten Lock Screen Password or PIN

If you've forgotten your Lock Screen Password or PIN, you'll need to reset your Kindle Fire to the factory settings. This erases your personal information, including your Lock Screen Password or PIN, Amazon account information, and downloaded content and apps. Your digital content is saved to the Cloud and may be downloaded again.

1. From the lock screen, slide the **Unlock Bar** from right to left.

2. Enter characters into the password/PIN field five times. After five attempts, you'll be prompted to reset your Kindle.

3. Tap **Reset**.

Set Parental Controls

You can enable **Parental Controls** to restrict access to the web browser, the Amazon store, the Cloud, and more.

1. Swipe down from the top of the screen to access **Quick Settings**, and tap **Settings**.

2. Tap **Open Kindle FreeTime** to open the Kindle Freetime app, or tap **On** next to **Parental Controls**.

3. With **Parental Controls** turned on, enter a password, confirm your password again, and then tap **Submit**. Once you've set the password, you can restrict one or more of these features:

    -   Web browsing

    -   Email, contacts, and Calendars app

    -   Social network sharing

    -   Camera

    -   Ability to purchase from the content stores such as the Amazon bookstore and Appstore

    -   Ability to play movies and TV shows from Amazon Instant Video

    -   Specific content types like Books or Apps

    -   Wireless connectivity

    -   Location-based services

After you turn on Parental Controls, a lock 🔒 icon appears at the top of the screen. The password is also required to turn off **Parental Controls**.

Forgotten Parental Controls Password

If you forget your Parental Controls password, you will need to reset your Kindle fire to the original factory settings. This will remove your personal information, including your settings for Parental Controls, Amazon account information, and downloaded content. However, your purchased content is saved to the Cloud and may be downloaded again.

1. Swipe down from the top of the screen to access **Quick Settings**, then tap **Settings**.

2. Tap **Device**.

3. Tap **Reset to Factory Defaults**, then tap **Reset**. Your device will restart.

Access Kindle FreeTime

If you have young children at home, you can create a personalized profile for each child, and restrict which books, apps, games and videos they may access. **Kindle FreeTime** allows you to temporarily switch your device's background color and fonts to a kid-friendly design. Children see only the apps and content you authorize them to see.

Parents can also set daily time limits for kids' tablet use, or restrict certain categories—like games and video—while leaving unlimited time for reading. They're blocked from using the Silk web browser and Kindle content stores or social features like Facebook. Your password is required to access FreeTime settings, to exit FreeTime, or enable or disable wireless connectivity.

A subscription service called **FreeTime Unlimited** provides unlimited access to kids' content from Disney, Nickelodeon, Sesame Street, PBS, and more for $2.99 a month. To get started, simply launch the Kindle FreeTime app, which comes preinstalled on your device.

To get started, you'll need to create a parental controls password and a profile for your child.

1. From **Home**, tap **Apps**, then tap **Kindle FreeTime**.

2. Tap **Get Started**.

3. Enter a password. This password is the same as your Parental Controls passwords, if you've created one.

    - **If you already have a Parental Controls password**: Enter your password, then tap Submit.

    - **If you don't have a Parental Controls password**: Create and confirm a password, then tap Continue.

4. From the **Add Child Profile screen**, select **Tap to set photo** to add a profile picture.

5. Enter your child's name, birthdate, and gender, then tap **Next**. You can create up to four child profiles. After setting up Kindle FreeTime, you can add content you've purchased to your child's profile and set up daily educational goals and time limits. A profile must have content to finish setting up Kindle FreeTime. (Profile information is used to customize the experience, but Amazon doesn't collect personally identifiable information.)

6. Tap Done to save your settings and create the profile.

Add or Remove Content From a Kindle FreeTime Profile

Only you can add or remove items in Kindle FreeTime.

1. From the **Parent Settings** page of **Kindle FreeTime**, tap **Manage Content & Subscription**.

2. Enter your Parental Controls password, then tap **Submit**.

3. Tap **Add Titles** to [Your Child]'s Library.

4. Tap the checkbox next to each title you want to add. To remove titles, uncheck the boxes beside each title. Movies and TV shows can only be deleted from outside Kindle FreeTime.

Subscribe to Kindle FreeTime Unlimited

Kindle FreeTime Unlimited is an optional monthly subscription offering thousands of books, apps, movies, and TV shows for children aged three to eight years old. Books, apps, movies and TV shows are refreshed periodically, and the content available to your child's profile doesn't display any ads, options for in-app purchases, or links to websites or social media like Facebook or Twitter.

1. To subscribe to Kindle Freetime Unlimited:

    a) From **Parent Settings** screen of Kindle FreeTime, tap **Manage Content & Subscription**.

    b) Enter your parental controls password, then tap **Submit**.

    c) Under Manage Subscription Content, tap **Subscribe** to Kindle FreeTime Unlimited and select a monthly subscription plan. Subscriptions start at $4.99 per month, and a discount of $2.99 for Amazon Prime subscribers.

To unsubscribe from Kindle FreeTime Unlimited, from the Parent Settings screen of Kindle FreeTime, tap Manage Content & Subscription. Under Manage Subscription Content, tap **Unsubscribe** from Kindle FreeTime Unlimited.

Set Daily Goals and Time Limits

In Kindle FreeTime, you can set a daily limit for total screen time, and daily time limits for your child to read, watch or play content and set educational goals, such as reading 20 minutes every day.

1. From the **Parent Settings** screen, tap **Daily Goals & Time Limits**.

2. Enter your Parental Controls password, then tap **Submit**.

3. Select the profile you want to update, and tap **On**. Choose different educational goals and time limits.

Add Photos From Facebook

If you've linked your Facebook account with your Kindle Fire, you can add photos from Facebook to your Cloud Drive and view them on your Kindle Fire.

1. From the **Home** screen, tap **Photos**.

2. Swipe from the left edge of the screen, and tap **Add Photos**.

3. Tap **Facebook**.

4. Tap **Add Facebook Photos**, then tap **OK**. Your photos from Facebook will be added to your Cloud Drive.

Add Photos From a Mobile Device or Your Computer

Follow the steps above for adding Facebook photos. At Step #3, instead of tapping Facebook, tap Mobile Device, PC or Mac, or Transfer through USB.

Share Photos

You can email photos and videos from your Kindle Fire—or post photos and videos to your Facebook or Twitter account.

1. From **Home**, tap **Photos**.

2. Swipe from the left edge of the screen, then select the categories under **Photos** or **Sources**.

3. Tap the photo or video you want to share.

4. Tap the **Share** icon.

*   To email the photo or video, tap **email**.

*   To post the photo or video to Facebook, tap **Facebook**. (Before sharing, you can tag people, add your location, and choose the audience for your photo.)

*   To post to Twitter, tap **Twitter**. Your tweet must be 140 characters or less.

If you're viewing multiple photos or videos in an album, tap the **Share** icon, select the photos or videos you want to share, and then tap **Facebook**, **Email**, or **More** to share multiple photos or videos. You can share up to 10 at a time.

Take Photos and Video

The camera on your Kindle Fire HDX can take photos and record video, and the documents can be automatically stored in Amazon's Cloud Drive. To open the camera, go to the **Home** screen, then tap **Photos**, then tap the **Camera** icon.

Switch to **Camera mode** or **Video mode**.

Take a picture. Tap the screen to focus on a particular area. Use the volume buttons on the back of your device to zoom in and out.

Record a video. A counter appears showing the length of time of the video.

Set Up Email, Contacts and Calendar

You'll need an email account to sync with the Email, Contacts, and Calendar apps on your Kindle Fire. You can add more than one account, which enables combined or single-account views in each of the apps.

The email app supports most services like Gmail, Outlook and Yahoo!, and will automatically populate the server settings during setup. For other email providers, you'll need to obtain the email settings from your provider.

To set up an email account:

1. From **Home** tap **Apps**, and then tap **Email**.

2. Enter your email address, then tap **Next**.

3. Enter the password for your email account, then tap **Next**.

4. If your email account isn't recognized, tap **Advanced Setup** to manually add your account.

TIP: If you use your Kindle Fire for viewing email, you should consider requiring a password to awaken your Kindle. Otherwise, anyone who picks up your Kindle could view your personal messages.

Use the Contacts App

The **Contacts** app lets you view, sync and edit your contacts list from your personal or business email account. When you set up your email account on your Kindle Fire, your contacts are automatically imported, and can be used by other apps and services installed on your Kindle Fire, such as Skype.

- **Open the Contacts app** – From **Home**, tap **Apps**, then **Contacts**.

- **Search for a contact** – Tap the **Search** icon in the **Options Bar** at the bottom of the screen, then enter text.

- **Add a contact** – Tap **New**.

- **Sync contacts from Facebook** – Swipe from the left edge of the screen, then tap **Settings**. Tap **Contacts General Settings**, then turn **On** the option to Sync Facebook Contacts.

Use the Calendar App

You can sync your calendars from Gmail, Yahoo!, Exchange, Outlook/Hotmail, and Facebook to your Kindle Fire.

- **Open the Calendar app** – From **Home**, tap **Apps**, then tap **Calendar**.

- **Change Calendar view** – Tap **Calendar** in the upper left corner of the app, then select **List**, **Day**, **Week** or **Month**.

- **Create an event** – Tap the **Menu** icon   , then tap **New Event**.

- **Add Facebook events** – If your Facebook account is linked to your Kindle Fire, you can add Facebook events to your calendar. Swipe from the left edge of the screen, then tap **Settings**. Turn on the option to **Sync Facebook Events.**

Redeeming Gift Cards or Promotional Codes

When you apply a Kindle promotional code or gift card to your account, it will automatically be applied to your next qualifying order. To redeem a promotional code or Amazon.com gift card:

1. On the product page, click **Enter a promotional code or gift card** below the **Buy** link

2. Enter the code and click **Apply**.

Conserve Your Battery

Battery life ranges from 10 to 18 hours depending on which functions you're using. Playing games and watching video consumes power at the fastest clip, while reading documents consumes less power.

Adjusting settings and turning off features of your Kindle Fire can help conserve your battery life between charging sessions.

- **Adjust notification settings.** Swipe down from the top of the screen to access **Quick Settings**. Tap **Settings**, then tap **Notifications & Quiet Time**. From the list, choose an application, or tap **Quiet Time** to disable notification alerts.

- **Lower screen brightness.** If you're indoors, particularly with subdued room lighting, you can probably tolerate less screen brightness in exchange for longer battery life. Swipe down from the top of the screen to access **Quick Settings**. Tap **Brightness**. Adjust the roller bar to lower your screen's brightness.

- **Turn off wireless**. If you don't need a wireless connection, turn off the Wi-Fi function to conserve power. Swipe down from the top of the screen to access **Quick Settings**. Tap **Wireless**. Tap the **On** button next to **Airplane mode**.

- **Use headphones**. You can enjoy high-fidelity sound by using headphones, which requires less power than the internal speakers. Plug headphones into the jack on the side of your Kindle fire.

- **Adjust screen timeout to less than 30 minutes**. Swipe down from the top of the screen to open **Quick Settings**. Tap **Settings**. Tap **Display & Sounds**, then tap **Display Sleep** to shorten the interval when your Kindle enters sleep mode while it's not being used.

- **Reduce frequency for the email app**. Swipe down from the top of the screen to open **Quick Settings**, then tap **Settings**. Tap **Email, Contacts, Calendars**. Select your email account, then tap **Inbox check frequency** to lengthen the interval your device checks for new messages.

Show Percentage of Battery Charge Remaining

The battery icon at the top of your screen shows the battery life or charging status. You can make your Kindle display the percentage of remaining battery charge to get a sense of how much power remains.

1. Swipe down from the top of the screen to open **Quick Settings**, then tap **Settings**.

2. Tap **Device**.

3. Tap the **On** button for **Show Battery Percentage in the Status Bar**.

4. The percentage of remaining battery life will appear to the left of the battery indicator.
   86% 🔋

If Your Battery Fails to Charge

For best results, use the USB cable and power adapter that came with your Kindle Fire. If the device fails to recharge, restart your Kindle Fire.

1. Press and hold the **Power** button for about 20 seconds until your device shuts down.

2. Wait about 20 seconds. Press the **Power** button again to turn on your device.

3. Leave your device connected to the power adapter until the battery icon in the **Status Bar** is filled completely.

Deregister Your Kindle Fire

If you'd like to switch the Amazon account associated with your Kindle—or you want to disable the purchasing of content from your Kindle—you can deregister your Kindle Fire. You can deregister from the device itself, or in the event of a lost or stolen Kindle, you can deregister from your computer.

From your device:

1. Swipe down from the top of the screen to reach **Quick Settings**, then tap **Settings**.

2. Tap **My Account**.

3. Tap **Deregister**.

From your computer:

1. Visit the **Manage Your Kindle** page at www.amazon.com/myk

2. Click **Manage Your Devices**.

3. Under Registered Kindles, click **Deregister**.

4. Confirm by clicking Deregister again.

After deregistering, you may register your Kindle with another Amazon account.

Changing the Time Zone

Your Kindle Fire automatically chooses the time zone, which determines the date and time displayed on your device. The current time is displayed on the Status Bar at the top. There is no option to adjust the date and time manually, but you can select a different time zone.

To change the time zone:

1. Swipe down from the top of the screen to display **Quick Settings**, then tap **Settings**.

2. Tap **Device**, then tap **Date & Time**.

3. Tap **Select Time Zone**, and then select your time zone from the list. The clock then displays the date and time for that zone.

Syncing Audiobooks, Videos and Games

If you buy a Kindle book that includes the Whispersync feature (not all books include it), you can switch back and forth between:

- Reading the book with your Kindle device or app

- Listening to the audiobook edition using your Kindle device or app

Amazon Instant Video also includes the Whispersync feature, so you can resume watching a video across your Kindles or compatible devices.

Manage Your Subscription Settings

1. You can make changes to your subscriptions to magazines, newspapers and blogs.

2. Visit Manage Your Kindle at www.amazon.com/myk

3. Under Your Kindle Account, click **Subscription Settings**.

   On the Subscription Settings page, click the **Actions** button next to the title, then you can:

   - Deliver past issues of subscription content to an eligible Kindle device or app.

   - Cancel a subscription

   - Download a title or issue of a subscription to your computer, then transfer it to your Kindle via USB cable.

   - Choose privacy preferences, whether to share your email address with subscription publishers.

Edit Device Names

The name of your device is set automatically by Amazon, but you can change the name of the device to make it more meaningful. For example, when my most recent Kindle Fire arrived in its box, Amazon named it "Steve's 7th Kindle." I changed the name to "Steve's Kindle HDX" so that I can distinguish it from my two other Kindle Fire devices purchased earlier.

The device name appears at the upper left corner of your Kindle Fire screen and on the **Manage Your Kindle** page. Here's how to edit the name of your device:

1. Visit Manage Your Kindle at www.amazon.com/myk

2. Click **Manage Your Devices**.

3. Click **Edit** beside the name of the device or app.

4. Enter the desired name and click **Update**.

Delete Items From Your Kindle Library

If you want to free up space on your Kindle device, you can tap its icon once, then tap **Remove From Device**. If you wish, you'll be able to send the item to your Kindle at a future point. By contrast, if you delete an item from your Kindle library, the action is permanent—you won't be able to download the item again unless you buy it again.

1. Visit Manage Your Kindle at www.amazon.com/myk

2. Locate the item you want to delete.

3. From the **Actions** drop-down menu, select **Delete from library**. Confirm by clicking **Yes**.

Hide Home Screen Recommendations

While you're using your Kindle Fire in portrait mode, you'll see personalized recommendations beneath the carousel on the home screen. For example, if a mystery book is displayed on your carousel, below the book cover you'll see four more similar books available for purchase, perhaps by the same author. If you're not interested in seeing these recommendations on your Home screen, you can dismiss them.

To hide individual recommendations of a specific book, press and hold the item, then tap **Not Interested**.

To hide all recommendations, swipe down from the top of the screen to access **Quick Settings**, then tap **Settings**. Tap **Applications**. Tap **Home** screen, then tap **Hide**.

In addition to these personalized recommendations based on items you've purchased before, the Kindle Fire displays **Special Offers & Sponsored Screensavers** on the lockscreen, visible when you awaken your device. You can remove these advertisements for a fee of $15 by visiting **Manage Your**

Kindle at www.amazon.com/myk . Under the heading **Manage Your Devices,** select your Kindle Fire device. Beside **Special Offers,** click **Edit,** then **Unsubscribe.**

Link to Facebook, Goodreads or Twitter

You can link your Kindle Fire to social networking sites to share your reading status, notes, book highlights, and book ratings. Plus, you can import your calendars, contacts and photos from your Facebook account.

Swipe down from the top of the screen to reveal **Quick Settings,** then tap **Settings.**

1. Tap **My Account.**

2. Tap **Social Network Accounts,** then tap Facebook, Twitter, or Goodreads.

3. Enter the account information for your social network, then tap **Done.**

Share Notes and Highlights

Your comments are automatically shared with the Goodreads community if you've linked your Kindle Fire to your Goodreads account. If you haven't linked your Kindle Fire to your Facebook or Twitter account—or you don't have a Goodreads account—you'll be prompted to connect your Kindle Fire to a social network before you can share notes and highlights.

To share your notes and highlights on Facebook, Twitter, or Goodreads:

1. While reading, press and drag to highlight the text you want to share.

2. Tap the **Share** icon.

3. Tap the **Add an optional note** field, then enter your comment.

4. Tap **Share** to share your comment with the Goodreads community. If you want to share to Facebook or Twitter, tap the checkboxes beside each social network, then tap **Share.**

11 ► VIEW PERSONAL DOCUMENTS, PHOTOS AND VIDEO

One of the strongest features of the Kindle Fire is its compact size. It's easy to tote around and, if you wish, it can often take the place of a laptop computer. If you're going to use your Fire frequently as an e-reader or productivity tool, taking advantage of Amazon's **Personal Documents Service** is a must. Although Amazon's Kindle books use a proprietary format—you need a Kindle (or a Kindle app) to read them—you can send virtually any kind of digital document to your Kindle using the Personal Documents Service.

You can use the Personal Documents Service along with your **Send-to-Kindle** email address. The email address is usually formatted as follows: [Your Name]@Kindle.com

If you're unsure of your Send-to-Kindle address, you can review it at Amazon's **Manage Your Kindle** web page at www.amazon.com/myk

Kindle Personal Documents Service

You can send documents to your Kindle using either the **Send to Kindle** application or from an email address you've authorized (this procedure is explained in the following section). Attach the document to an email and send it to your **Send-to-Kindle email address**, which is a unique email address automatically assigned by Amazon.

Documents that you send to your Send-to-Kindle email address are stored in the Cloud and synced across all compatible Kindle devices and reading apps. The documents appear in the **Docs** library on your Kindle Fire.

1. To change your Send-to-Kindle email address, visit **Manage Your Kindle** at www.amazon.com/myk and click **Personal Documents Settings**.

2. Under **Send-to-Kindle email address**, click **Edit**.

3. Enter the new address, and click **Update**.

If your document needs to be converted to Kindle's .azw format, enter "convert" in the email's subject line.

Your Approved Personal Document Email List

Your Kindle can only receive documents from email addresses you've approved. The regular email address registered with your Amazon account is already added to the approved list.

To edit your **Approved Personal Document Email list**:

1. Visit **Manage Your Kindle** at www.amazon.com/myk and click **Personal Document Settings**.

2. Under **Approved Personal Document Email list**, select **Add a new approved email address**.

3. Enter the new email address and click **Add Address**.

Converting Documents

One of the best features of the Personal Documents Service is that it can automatically convert most common document formats to the Kindle format, called AZW. You don't have to know the technical details, it just works. Then once the document is on your Kindle, you can use many of the functions available with Kindle documents—you can make annotations, change the font, adjust the text size, and so forth. To convert your documents, enter the word **Convert** in the subject line of the email.

TIP: Don't use Personal Documents Service for commercial purposes, such as sending out a commercial newsletter. It's against Amazon's terms of service, and that's why it's called the Personal Documents Service.

Transfer Personal Documents Via USB Cable

Let's say you want to transfer a document from your computer to your Kindle via USB cable, and you need to convert the document to Kindle's .azw format. Before you can accomplish this, you'll need to change your Send-to-Kindle email address to the name [your-name]@free.kindle.com and then enter "convert" in the subject line of your email.

1. To download the converted document to your computer, follow the instructions Amazon puts in the email.

2. Choose your desktop, then click **Save**.

3. Connect your Kindle to your computer with the USB cable. (On a Windows computer, navigate to the Kindle by browsing **My Computer**. (On Macs, the Kindle will appear on your desktop.)

4. Click on the **Kindle** to browse the Kindle's drive.

5. Drag your document from your desktop and drop it into the **Documents** folder of the Kindle drive.

6. Eject your Kindle device and unplug the USB cable.

Supported File Types for Kindle Personal Documents Service

The following file types can be automatically converted to the Kindle format .azw by sending them in an email with "convert" in the subject line:

Microsoft Word (.doc, .docx)

HTML (.html, .htm)

RTF (.rtf)

Text (.txt)

JPEG (.jpeg, .jpg)

Kindle Format (.mobi, .azw)

GIF (.gif)

PNG (.png)

BMP (.bmp)

PDF (.pdf)

'Send to Kindle' Application

Another way to send documents to your Kindle is by using the **Send to Kindle** application, a free program you can install on your computer. With it, you can send content such as word-processing documents, news articles, blog posts and other content to your Kindle.

The Send-to-Kindle application is quite efficient and easy to use, and it automatically converts documents to the Kindle format.

Download the program by visiting www.amazon.com/gp/sendtokindle and following the instructions. After entering your Amazon email address and password, click **Register**. If you own more than one Kindle device, you can select which device(s) will receive the documents.

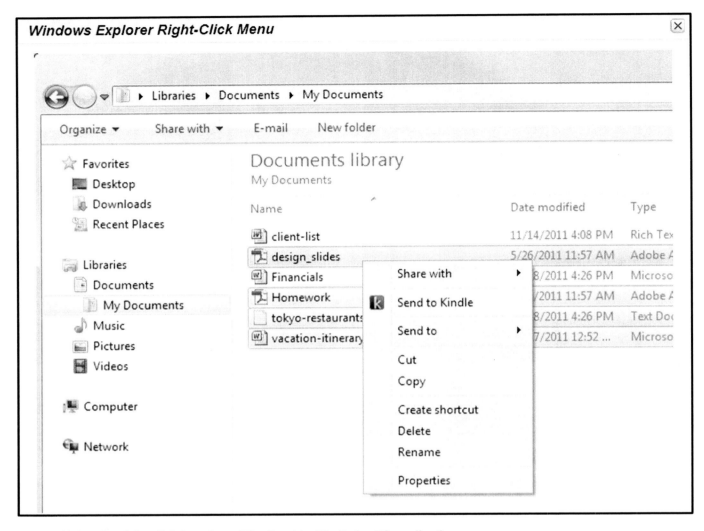

Above: Using the right-click function of the Send-to-Kindle for PC application

Send-to-Kindle is also available as a browser extension for the Chrome and Firefox Web browsers.

Download From the Cloud

All of your Kindle content is saved to the Cloud and available for download to your Kindle Fire. Let's imagine that you want to download a previously purchased Kindle book to your Kindle Fire.

1. From the **Home** screen, tap **Books** to open its content library.

2. Tap **Cloud** (instead of **Device**) to display the books you own that haven't been downloaded to your Kindle Fire.

3. Tap the **book** image to download it to your device. Items that have been downloaded to your Kindle Fire have a check mark in the lower right corner of the cover image. Items stored in the Cloud do not have a check mark.

4. Tap the book to open it.

Transfer Personal Documents and Photos Via USB

You can transfer your photos and personal videos from your computer to your Kindle Fire with the micro-USB cable that came in the box, or upload your photos or videos to the Cloud Drive using free software from Amazon. Visit www.kindle.com/support/downloads

When you connect your Kindle Fire to a Windows computer, your device appears as a storage drive as in the illustration below. This enables you to "sideload" music, book and other documents directly from your computer's hard drive.

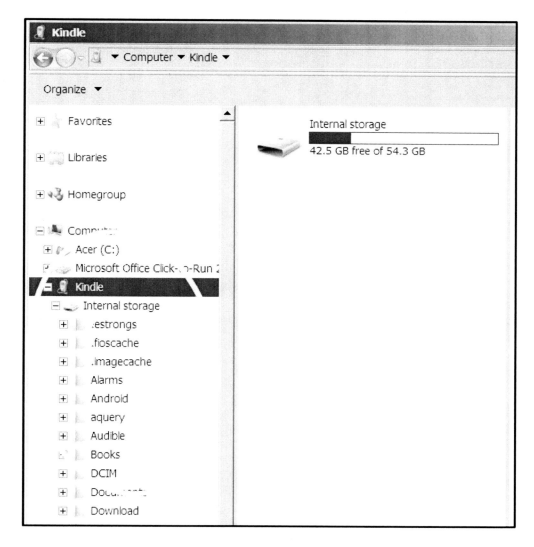

Above: The Kindle Fire, connected to a Windows computer with the included micro-USB cable, appears as a storage device.

Personal photos and videos that you load onto your Kindle Fire are handled differently than media you buy from Amazon. While your Amazon video content goes straight to your Video Library, your personal videos are accessed from the **Photos** content library.

1. From your computer, locate the content you want to transfer from your computer to your Kindle Fire.

2. Connect your Kindle Fire to your computer with the micro-USB cable. (On a Windows computer, your Kindle Fire will appear in the **My Computer** folder; on a Mac, the Kindle will appear on your desktop.)

3. Open the Kindle Fire folder (titled Kindle) on your computer, and then open the Internal storage folder.

4. Drag and drop the file you want to transfer into the appropriate Kindle folder. For photos, the destination folder would be **Pictures**. For video, the destination is the **Movies** folder. There are also folders for **Audiobooks**, **Books**, **Documents**, and **Music**.

Download Photos and Personal Videos From the Cloud

You can download your photos and personal videos from your Cloud Drive account to your Kindle Fire.

1. From **Home**, tap **Photos**.

2. Swipe from the left edge of the screen, then tap **Cloud Drive Files**. Photos or videos stored in your Cloud Drive appear here.

3. Press and hold a photo or video, then tap **Download**.

4. Swipe from the left edge of the screen, then tap **Device** to see your downloaded photo or video.

Amazon allows 5 GB of free storage in your Cloud account. To start using your Cloud drive, visit **Manage Your Amazon Cloud Drive** at www.amazon.com/clouddrive/manage

Printing Documents

If you have a printer that supports wireless printing, you can print Word, Excel, PowerPoint or PDF documents. Printing isn't supported for Kindle format (.azw) documents.

Before printing, you'll need to download a plugin from the Amazon App store to your Kindle Fire. Download the plugin compatible with your printer:

- **Epson:** www.amazon.com/dp/B00ENB2CSK

- **HP:** www.amazon.com/dp/B00EDUTGB2

- **Canon:** www.amazon.com/dp/B00E19FB28

- **Samsung:** www.amazon.com/dp/B00DMZ3AM0

- **Ricoh:** www.amazon.com/dp/B00FAX29AG

After downloading the plugin, turn on your printer and ensure it's connected to Wi-Fi, and follow these steps:

1. Press and hold the document you wish to print, then tap **Print.**

2. Select your printer from the list, tap **OK**, then tap **Connect**. If your printer isn't listed, tap + to search for more printers.

Index

DATE DUE

AG 1 3 '74			
DE 1 0 '14			
AG 0 2 '15			
SE 0 9 '15			
			PRINTED IN U.S.A.

CPSIA information can be obtained at www.ICGtesting.com
Printed in the USA
LVOW09s2347130514

385614LV00018B/770/P

9 781936 560189